THE QUIET TIDES
OF BORDEAUX

In a quiet suburb of Bordeaux, France, memories from the last century haunt the thoughts of a retired, lonely widow, night after night. Time is running out for this former schoolmistress: she opens up to a stranger, the narrator, to have her story serve as a lesson for the next generation. In the process, she is led to revisit a wartime decision, involving a forbidden romance, deeply rooted in wolf-pack psychology. In spite of her upbringing and her redemption in her career, she comes to question her sacrifice. In the end, her ordeal will be acknowledged by a coincidence.

Love is so short, and forgetting is so long.

— Pablo Neruda, Twenty Poems of Love, XX, 1924

J. L. F. Lambert

THE QUIET TIDES OF BORDEAUX

–8Θ8Θ8–

Introductory Note

The words and documents reproduced in this story have been approved for publication by Madame H*** (note dated 31 Aug. 2011, witnessed by her step-granddaughter). This author is fully obliged to Madame H***. He is equally grateful to his companion, BrendaLee Wilson, for her thorough editing contribution, and to his friend Yanic Bernard for his logistical assistance. He also wishes to thank the following people: the mayor of Eyrans, Bernard Bailan; the city archivist of Lourdes, Jean-François Labourie; a former child evacuee from Nantes, Gérard Piquet; a former Lourdes guide, Paulette Abadie-Douce; a former neighbour of Madame H***'s sisters, Éric Décombe; the author of *Bordeaux, mon amour*, Erich Schaake; and, for the English edition, Dania Sheldon, Sylvia Shawcross, and Olga Zuyderhoff.

–8Θ8Θ8–

Lambert, J. L. F. (Jean Louis François), Toulouse 1948-
The Quiet Tides of Bordeaux (an adaptation from the French of *Paisible Garonne* by the same author).

Maps, drawings, and notes by the author; drawings (except six) inspired by photographic sources from Madame H***, Google Earth, Internet (incl. Bundesarchiv and delcampe.net [CAP]), B. Bailan, J.-F. Labourie, and G. I. P. and L. Chatagneau postcards. Photo credits: the author, B. L. Wilson, and anonymous from Madame H*** and P. Abadie-Douce via G. Piquet. (2eS Txt Gmd 125 vsp 105 mrg 2 175 075; 2eH Txt TNR 12 vsp 110 mrg 2 175 075)

Title confirmed by Library and Archives Canada 2014.01.31
2nd edition, reprint
ISBN 978-0-9936926-8-0 (softcover)
ISBN 978-0-9936926-9-7 (hardcover)
ISBN 978-0-9947728-0-0 (ebook)

France, Aquitaine, 20th cent., Blaye, Bordeaux, Étauliers, Lourdes, Royan, Saintes, Customs, Determinism, Conditioning, Conformity, Religious differences, World war II, Refugees, Evacuee children, German occupation, Education, Health-and-boarding centres, Trade schools, Love, Loneliness, Memory

The Main Characters

Micheline (Michou) Ponthier, a career teacher, 1916-
    Her father, Louis Gabriel, a hardware dealer, 1869-1945;
    her mother, Jeanne, 1880-1954; her sisters: Aline, 1898-1992;
    Marcelle, 1900-52; Cécile, 1902-97; her brother, Rémy,
    a railway employee, 1901-83; her cousin, J.; another cousin

Jacques Celse, a country doctor, 1910 (?)-(see Post-Epilogue)
    His father, a minister; his mother, J.; his brother and his sister-
    in-law; his sister, ?-1929

Laurent Hébert, a career teacher, 1898-1992
    His father, Alix, a tanning craftsman, 1866-1907; his mother,
    Léonie, 1875-1960; his first spouse, Georgette, 1901-50;
    his daughter, Paulette, a pharmacist, 1924-97; his son-in-law,
    Pierre, a manager, 1922-2008; his grandchildren: Laure (Loly),
    1948-; Yann, 1952-2010; Gildas, 1955-

Illustrations

Correspondence

To Madame H***

Map of the Gironde Estuary
(southwestern France)

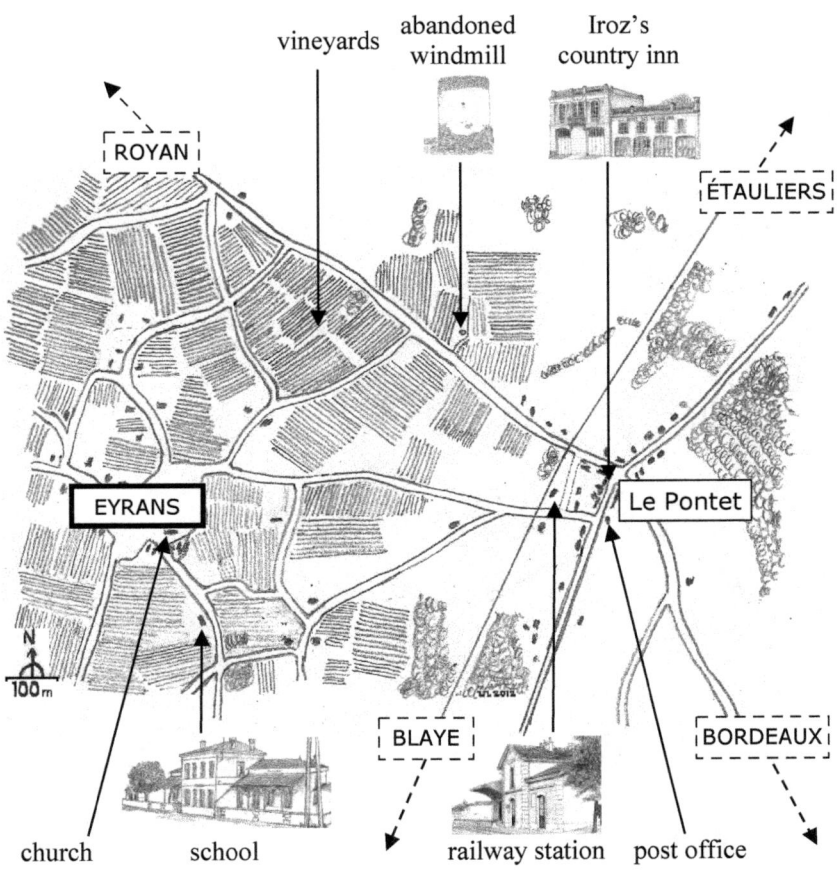

vineyards   abandoned windmill   Iroz's country inn

ROYAN

ÉTAULIERS

EYRANS

Le Pontet

N
100m

BLAYE

BORDEAUX

church   school   railway station   post office

Along the Blayais Marchland (map)

PART I

1

When you get off the tram at the Palmer Stop in Cenon, on a hill above Bordeaux, in southwestern France, just before the La Morlette shopping centre, and you walk down Charles-de-Foucauld, a narrow, straight, one-way street, you find yourself in a cream-coloured neighbourhood of single-family homes crouching behind low walls and hedges. It is a frozen world of silence and cleanliness, where empty streets, lined with closed shutters and pulled curtains, run along deserted yards and gardens. A small, hurried housewife, a car suddenly racing by parked vehicles, or a moving djellabah shape, makes the stroller wonder if those were apparitions, once peace and quiet have returned. It is the same picture on every street, each stretching towards a multilane motorway with a monotonous hum that numbs the mind.

There was no such neighbourhood here sixty years ago, at the end of WWII. Large wooded estates, held by the Bordeaux gentry, a legacy from the claret and triangular slave-and-sugar trades, had sprawled in all their splendour for centuries along the escarpment overlooking the Garonne River, and Bordeaux itself, with its harbour in the shape of a moon crescent. Time and again, orchestras and garden parties had resounded through those parks. But by the end of the German occupation, the palaces had suffered injury. Properties such as the Palmer and La Morlette estates had to be put up for sale. The Palmer estate was bought by the municipality and then resold, along with its centenary oak trees, to housing developers as reconstruction was spurred by new, post-war laws, and people's attachment to the land began to loosen.

The eleven-hectare La Morlette estate was turned over to the Ministry of Education, which turned it into a young women's training centre. This project was managed right after the war by Micheline Ponthier, a young and dynamic schoolteacher whose name might have been predestined. Three years later, she was put in charge of the new centre. She was barely thirty, with a full life already behind her—one that new duties could help forget.

Proceeding along Charles-de-Foucauld Street and a little beyond, one reaches the abode of Mademoiselle Ponthier, who has since become Madame Hébert. Her white bungalow with a garage attached under the same red roof is barely visible, behind a small, beige wall and a dark bay-leaf hedge. In the back, on the garden side, are a sunroom and a spacious living room that appear to have been added on. Monsieur and Madame Hébert spent many happy years here together, watching their rosebushes grow. Monsieur Hébert, first-name Laurent, liked to sit on the little bench along the garden path, after his stroke.

Many years earlier, the Minister of Education's deputy had ended his inaugural speech for the training centre, embracing Miss Ponthier, declaring: "Mademoiselle, you are a very fortunate woman." And indeed, four years later she compounded her luck by marrying Monsieur Hébert, her counterpart from the young men's training college. At the beginning of their courtship, this widowed colleague had invited her to the movies "with no hidden motive." During the projection he had simply taken her hand.

Madame Hébert lives alone now. She is 93, and even though her occupations have become quite simple, they can easily keep her busy the whole day, but she sometimes manages to meet old friends to play Scrabble.

Her bedroom is the size of two little rooms that have been joined together. A prie-dieu, a precious legacy from her parents, now stands between the windows, where the dividing wall used to be. When she wakes up in the morning, Madame Hébert faces a large rococo mirror, framed with multiple smaller mirrors reflecting both the walls and the ceiling. It was quite a remarkable wedding gift. It might remind her of a mirror in her bedroom when she was a celibate schoolmistress. That one would reflect, from across her room, the oil refineries on fire in the middle of the night, at the mouth of the Garonne River, on the Gironde Estuary. Their bombardments had her running to the loo.

Madame Hébert's career was sealed from the moment she received her primary-school diploma. From that day in June 1928, when she was not yet twelve years of age, she had a plan she would never veer from, thanks to her teacher in Étauliers, her hometown, inland from the right bank of the Gironde. When she speaks of it, she spreads her arms as if to lay her life's foundation on the table, clearly and firmly.

This school scene in Étauliers is to be the starting point of her memoirs relating her professional life. She is determined to have them written down, all the more so because she needs to have her personal memories put in order. After her career ended and her husband died, she penned these thoughts:

> My memory is a labyrinth out of which I cannot escape.
> I need Ariadne's thread to take me out of this devious maze,
> and finally find peace.

Madame Hébert knows this statement is in contradiction with her peaceful neighbourhood. But she insists unequivocally, in spite of all she has done for young people, she still has "something to offer to future generations … on the psychological and historical levels."

Madame Hébert pauses ... as if her mind were going on a tangent.... Yes, she is back in Étauliers ... her sisters are teaching her to read at age five ... *Little Poucet* ... and to sew. She complains about the cold when her mother wakes her up for school. Still no running water, no electrical power.... "Mother! Quick, my stockings!" Then she falls prey to both panic and self-control: "I'm going to be late! I'm going to be late!" Pale-faced and out of breath, she makes it to school, but is stopped dead in her tracks by the teacher's eyes and finger: "You haven't had your breakfast! Go back home!" ... After school she retreats into the cool basement and scoops cream from the milk kept there to spread onto her bread, and grates chocolate over it—such a treat!

But soon she leaves her dolls and rabbits behind to enter a boys' school, where girls have just been allowed to study, in Blaye, on the Gironde Estuary, less than twenty kilometres away. She is taken in by an old widow living on a dreary street, who serves nothing but frugal dinners to Micheline and two schoolmates, Raymonde and Jeanne, before they go and weep at night with their noses stuck to the window. Her father comes to Blaye to collect goods Saturday mornings for his shop from the port's docks, and to buy fish at the market. He takes her out the first Saturday only to have her pattering behind him, begging him to take her back. In the end, he gives in, and she is allowed to come home on weekends. But on Monday mornings, as she is led to the railway station, it is the same scene, trying to negotiate with her mother: "I promise you, I'll sweep the kitchen floor, I'll wash the dishes, I'll do anything you want." Blaye—a four-year exile.

Next, Bordeaux. At Cheverus Primary High, the girls were in constant fear of being labelled bad pupils. The comments of that era still ring in her ears. They would rain haphazardly on the class: "My poor girl, your brain is made of gelatine!" On Sundays, Micheline would take refuge at her cousins' in La Bastide, on the right bank of the Garonne. And later, at the age of sixteen, when she boarded at the women's teachers' college, on the left-bank suburb of Caudéran, her outings were only allowed under the supervision of her guardians *in loco parentis*, a night watchman and his wife from downtown Bordeaux. This generous couple came to take her out once a month, to round off her Catholic education. Eventually, Micheline could leave the boarding school a few more hours a month, thanks to a Protestant schoolmate by the name of Gilberte who took her home to visit her parents, and her younger brother, Guillaume.

After graduating from teachers' college, Micheline found herself teaching in a primary school in the countryside, at Eyrans, within a stone's throw of her birthplace, Étauliers. The year was 1936. She cannot remember her twentieth birthday. What fill her eyes now, instead, are maps hanging from the walls … the children's smocks and clogs … purple ink in the porcelain inkpots … logs to bring in from the storehouse to light the fire half an hour before class … the stove pipe running across the ceiling…. And teaching three forms[*] in the same room….

No, really, nothing was pointing to a distinguished career—in a mansion.

*

Madame Hébert is proud of the mirror in her bedroom. Many of her staff and trainees clubbed together to present it to her when she married, but far be it from her to show conceit. Her faith demands humility, it keeps her on the right path. This does not mean that Madame Hébert does not pay attention to her appearance, for guests. She does it effortlessly, naturally, twirling her thick silver hair into a coil, somewhat loosely so it does not accentuate the long features of her face more than necessary. An unobtrusive necklace, and one or two rings,

---

[*] North American English: grades.

tastefully chosen together with a blouse and a jacket, will distract from her canes and walker.

Madame Hébert's day fills up quickly, with her household chores, her insurance forms, the follow-up to her donations to charities, and other administrative and medical business, nothing very complicated really, she knows this. Her afternoon is devoted to resting, after her homecare worker has left. She lies down in an electrically reclining armchair in front of the TV, in the living room. After a few minutes of National Assembly debates, she is fast asleep. This type of nap is a dry run for her, she can tell, especially at the beginning, when she gently melts away into unconsciousness. She wonders sometimes whether this is how she will pass on. Her faith sustains her more than ever today, now that she is about to be rejoined, God willing, with her beloved husband. Every now and then, especially in times of setbacks, she feels under siege, and even defeated. However never, ever, has she given in to doubt, for this just cannot to be done. Still, true to herself, she will get to the bottom of things. In spite of the religious volumes in her half-dozen bookcases; in spite of the lectures, the pilgrimages to Lourdes and to the Holy Land; and in spite of the televised rosaries and church services, she admits to being rather ignorant and unable to build an image of the 'other side' for herself. Silence, then, fills the room.... She purses her lips ... barely moves her chin forward ... and stares out into the beyond ... while the pupils of her eyes mirror the darkness of the abyss ... an unfathomable abyss.

*

Étauliers—once again.... The Ponthier town shop ... with its ironmongery, grocery, and haberdashery ... an Ali Baba cave set right between Main Street and Church Street ... between two little bridges ... a moat-like brook flowing along its walls—1924.... A room, a bedroom ... her bedroom ... in a maze of nine bedrooms ... with exhalations of carbide and turpentine snaking their way up the stairs.... Sleep is not coming ... darkness is all around.... And so is a presence ... a dark presence that is not a presence.... A vacuum in the mist of the void ... boundless.... Up to where?... Endless ... limitless ... on and on ... for eternity.... Darkness everywhere, to infinity ... calling ... sucking in ... undoing ... tearing off.... Emptiness and solitude—unbearable.... The unknown ... the total unknown, with no point of reference, no landmark.... Time does not exist.... All is still, motionless.... And so are her eyes.... Two wide, dark eyes stare where space, the room, infinity come pouring in.... Two round eyes, wide open, imploring ... desperately probing ... probing far away ... light years away, out there.... And a mouth, her mouth, ajar, frozen stiff.... Nothing coming through.... The 'I' has no place there ... it dissolves.... A scream tears the night—her sisters in their nightgowns rush to the rescue, "Michou, Michou...."

The episode recedes.... But then, later on, when her teacher moves on from "the causes and the roots" of the Great War, Michou is brought back to emptiness, the emptiness of the universe: the earth, the sun, the planets, the stars.... "How many planets are there? ... What are their names?" And the stars ... millions of stars to imagine, to conceive of ... and to find compatible with an array of questions and answers ... compatible with the catechism that resounds all around the church, from pillar to pillar, every Thursday, Thursday after Thursday: "What is God? ... How many persons are there in God?... Where is God?... He is everywhere. Therefore He is here.... God created everything...."

Stars.... Infinity.... Night.... The next bout of vertigo spins again through the night! "Michou, Michou, don't weep, we are here...." The Alpha and the Omega merge again; she opens her eyes.... Being and Nothingness are here, palpable, within her, she feels them....

The Ponthier family shop, Étauliers

She remembers becoming aware that she was an 'accident'. She was born after her father's medical discharge from the war, after he and her mother had ceased to conceive children fourteen years earlier, in 1902. "One more" ... that is, an addition to the three sisters and a maid, and one lone brother.... The maid was only thirteen when the father hired her; she had high cheekbones and stayed for nearly thirty years. But Micheline was still unaware of another form of chance—or was it destiny?—that kept her safely from the Spanish flu.

When she did occasionally take ill, she did not want them to call the doctor—only the teacher and the priest could clarify all this for her. And so, on it went, Thursday after Thursday, week after week, she made the priest's dogmas her own, reminding her of her place and showing her the logic of it....

Michou took her first communion in 1927. She remembers it to this day: it was around the time Thérèse de Lisieux was canonized. She can see herself, with the other little girls, throwing rose petals in front of the procession of the Blessed Sacrament.

*

All of this is lying around, here and there, in two or three rooms, in photo albums, in envelopes, and in shoeboxes. There are no photos of Micheline as a baby, nor of her first communion. She still feels a sense of loss—to this day. Black-and-white photos of her appear only after several pages of her sisters posing, first only one, Aline, then two, with Marcelle, and later all three of them, with Cécile, wearing muslin flower dresses, holding musical instruments or showing off wristwatches. Photos of their parents are rare—they were married at seventeen and twenty-eight; they look like bronze sculptures, the father sporting a walrus moustache and a boater hat, and the mother nearly always sitting. The brother, Rémy, appears in the albums only when he is around age fifteen, posing placidly, as if for a painting, with his Moroccan guest in a Spahi uniform; on other occasions, another stranger stands behind him, both of them stiff and inexpressive. Rémy's 1941 ID shows his height as 1.61m tall.*

Other pictures, of the grandchildren and great-grandchildren of Madame Hébert's husband, need to be filed. Some lie right there, on the dining room table; she walks by them every day. She will organize them soon in the new albums ready and waiting. She likes to see her great-grandchildren smile at her—it feels good to be loved.

Madame Hébert spends a good deal of time with her house help. She likes these young women. 'Young' in a manner

---

* 5 feet 3⅓ inches.

of speaking—it is all relative. These mature women descend from the generations of young women she guided with so much devotion. She cannot help but observe and assess them, in her own way, always as the principal of a training college. It takes place most of the time in the kitchen, a small room with orange walls from the sixties, where barely four people can sit under the gaze of a crucifix. She listens to her helpers, sometimes looking over the rim of her spectacles, with her piercing almond-shaped eyes.

The other day, she had a good discussion on fasting, with Fadila, the Moroccan helper, the one who parks her white Mercedes in front of the little gate, and does the morning chores. Madame Hébert likes to learn about Islam, it is a beautiful thing, and she says so as she bows her head. She is doing her best to practice tolerance, above all. Religion does not kill; on the contrary, it draws people together, and the proof of this is her conversations with Fadila. It is through Christ that she can accept the other. When France was liberated, she was appointed to Purge Commissions and disciplinary committees concerning religious interference in the educational system. This may be how Madame Hébert was able to create a new picture of Catholicism and tolerance for herself.

Madame Hébert now embodies tolerance itself: "I say, Yann, if you are happy with her…." For Yann, the eldest of her grandsons, had made up his mind to leave his wife for another one; it had been a question of happiness, a matter of health. And now, she has to make up her mind on the protocol for the photos in the albums. She wants to set them out in her own way, before passing them on to her grandchildren. "And after, well … they can burn them…."

To unscramble her memory, and maybe to match her husband's biography and dot the i's of her own life story, Madame Hébert had decided to hire a 'ghostwriter', but the final product failed to satisfy her: one hundred and one pages for a life, her life, filled with emptiness and clichés. She wrote a few comments in the margins. Each time she leafs through it, she wants to change the phrases, cut out the repetitions, and possibly get rid of the administrative jargon. But something else makes her sigh. Everything is there, except what is not. It should all be redone. But then, when would she find the time to file the photos in the albums? She knows she does not have many years left, and the thought of it keeps her from getting hold of herself and make decisions.

It is not always easy to identify the turning points of a life, the moments when a decision or resolution sows sorrow, bliss, or freedom. Her memoirs, for example, relate the impotence she felt at the time of the student revolts of 1968 and 1972. Had her lack of action been a matter of tolerance, irresolution, or rather, the result of some political scheme on the part of her male counterparts?

When the day comes to an end, when it is evening and she returns to her bedroom, tired and alone, before it all becomes dark again, she has no trouble blocking out the echoes of her past life. Rather, it is at night, when she wakes up, her shoeboxes a few paces away, that everything comes back to her.

* *

2

Madame Hébert often wakes up at night. It could be that the house is too quiet—and empty—since Laurent's passing. Emerging from nowhere, a drift of consciousness reminds her where she is laying, in her bed, as she recaptures in her mind the layout of the house.... No, Laurent is not with her anymore.... But his photos, certificates, and gifts form a trail from one room to the next: hadn't he promised he would be with her forever?

All is tidy; everything sits where it belongs, steeping in the dark, humid emptiness of the house. The night sometimes feels endless, especially after the middle of the night, during the twenty-fifth hour, before Madame Hébert finally surrenders to sleep. She changes position ... relieves a hip ... then her back ... in search of wellness ... of a state conducive to sleep. She thinks of a couple of routine tasks for the upcoming day, but her mind often returns to her youth, or rather, to an image of peace, almost always in sunshine—the latter, a detail she does not linger over. The image takes shape after she has had a sensation of letting go, of being taken over, permeated, cajoled. These moments with no beginning and no end are known only to her. This kind of escape has no discernible connection with what actually preoccupies her. When her mind clears on the following day, she will lift up her chin to describe the process.

Photo: anonymous, copy by J. L. F. Lambert, courtesy of M. H***

Micheline as a White Beret
Lourdes, 1933

As she drifts out of consciousness, a view through a wide-open window at her parents' home may come to her, almost automatically. She had taken refuge in the attic with a book at the end of a summer day. A vaguely fresh smell was hovering over the village and time seemed to stand still, as just before the angelus bell was about to toll. She had caught sight of a huge, lone cart, down below, slowly passing by on Main Street, the road to St. James of Compostela, carrying young men with their bare legs dangling from the top of overflowing hay. What emerged from this picture was not just a sense of labour and achievement—as one would have felt further to the north, by the ancient Protestant fortified ports of Royan and La Rochelle—, it was also the knowledge of a well-deserved rest, or even gaiety, coming up. Beyond this age-old picture, one could literally touch the status quo of tradition and the guarantee that nothing would change.

This may be why at times Madame Hébert lets out a sigh in her bed, and turns over. Days, weeks, and years overlap, making a mess of it. There are too many images to deal with and nothing to choose from, in the future. She tries to huddle somewhere in this maze of memories, just for the night; she will deal with the rest later. The depressing times spent in boarding schools outweigh the few good times of her youth, and when her memories resurface as words, there are no adverbs of intensity. She is searching, in spite of herself, moving slowly, little by little, towards her big question mark, another refuge. She reviews an old decision of hers, from all possible angles, and takes solace in justifying it religiously, again and again.

Yes, such was, and still is, her lot.

*

After she had attended teachers' college and taught a series of *practicums*, the sky had opened up above Micheline with the glaring sun of 1936, yes, July 1936. She breathed with relief and hope, her schooling was over, and she had graduated.

Madame Hébert relaxes, she may be going back to sleep....

Right—it was the end of that July. She had left with her mates for San Sebastian, in the Spanish Basqueland. She recalls the motorcoach ... full of girls ... supervised by the driver and the organizer ... their arrival at the hotel ... and the comings-and-goings between the rooms....

Far from her French village, in a foreign-sounding metropolis, Micheline was now part of the world. News coming from the Rhineland, Tunisia, and Abyssinia had aroused neither hate nor interest, in spite of thunderous wireless reports. Here in Spain, the girls took all this in with the same indifference, as they had in France. But then shots were fired, right on their first night, and the girls were packed back into their coach. They waved a flag put together with blue, white, and red clothes, and claimed French neutrality at checkpoints—with two refugees hiding under their seats. Back in Bordeaux, nobody believed them, but it did not matter: this first summer of emancipation made her discover a world where one could feel alive.

*

Micheline's first posting was to a rural primary school, in Eyrans, halfway between Étauliers and Blaye. She had barely moved into her flat above the little school, on the heights overlooking the hamlet of Le Pontet, when she was given a practical exam to confirm her appointment. She left the classroom and rushed back up to her room to fetch chairs for the inspector and her two assistants. The exam went like clockwork: she taught geography by making shapes with modelling clay on a blue board resting on her desk.

At just twenty years of age, she had settled down and was paying back her education and contributing to her pension plan. Micheline launched her career with method and efficiency. She had to teach the three girls' forms concurrently in the same classroom—one pre-primary and two primary years, amounting to a total of forty pupils. She could not afford any slippage in the curricula. The mechanics of her system made her feel secure, and this is precisely how routine and weariness crept in, the first two years, blending them into one another. She did receive some moral support from her older colleague who taught the intermediate levels and lodged in the other flat with his wife, in the main block of the school.

Pupils, parents, faces, a trait, a lock of hair in the wind— nothing, no detail, no triviality comes out of this whirl, except for the morning when the stove pipe broke and fell down onto the desks, just before the children were to enter the classroom. This prompted Micheline to organize the first of many discovery hikes that included the picking of plants, recorded in each child's notebook for the signature of the parents. The ABC drill is the only thing left still ringing in her ears ... to the rhythm of her heartbeat ... in the quiet of the night....

The Eyrans primary school

Fortunately, she could join her family on Sundays, and at Christmas and Easter. Étauliers was only a twenty-minute bicycle ride away. Sitting around the table with her parents, her sisters, and an occasional guest, she would forget her isolation. Everybody would talk about everything, in French, and in a patois that made one smile, especially when a village elder, 'refreshed' with wine soup, would recount the Great War to travelling salesmen.

Back in Eyrans, she would retreat to her room above the school. The emptiness she had felt when entering her flat for the first time appeared to have dissolved. Nowadays, Madame Hébert does not make an issue of this turning point in her life, the instant when in a single glance she had sized up the scanty contents of her room, the bare walls echoing each of her steps. Toiling away day after day, she did not have time to sense the return of emptiness. But gradually, week after week, alone in her room, as the night was advancing and the clock from the ground floor marked out the hours, Micheline would become Michou again, another Michou, the one who had made her way in the world and who wondered whether her yearnings to be a professional teacher had not led her into a blind alley. As she took tally of her well-established sisters in Étauliers, and of her brother now settled into a position with the railways in Paris, she could count herself their equal. But the fact that they were all unmarried like her made her feel uneasy.

Weeks would resume on Mondays, with the same drills, the same motions, the same faces, the same words, the same walls. The children would enter the classroom, singing, at 8:30 a.m. A case of morals was expounded, the elements of a sentence were analyzed on the blackboard, followed by reading, dictation, arithmetic, and the rest, alternating with game periods, such as cut-out cardboard letters, to keep the unsupervised forms busy. At noon, some pupils would stay, have their snacks, and play in the courtyard. Classes would resume at 1:30 p.m. and go on until 4:30 p.m., with a half-hour break, as in the morning. It was the same waltz on the following days, except Thursdays and Sundays, the same acrobatics, the same juggling with three forms, while standing on her feet for six hours.

At night, after class, it felt good to let fresh air swirl around her head as she walked down the slope, between the vineyards, to get her milk at a farmhouse, by the restaurant of Le Pontet's country inn. Looking at her, one could have said that she was sucking in the breeze from the ocean. On occasion, she let herself look out of the corner of her eye at women carrying bundles of firewood on their backs, lonely widows of men who fell in the Great War. With her bottle of fresh milk, Micheline would go back up to the school, cook dinner on the coal stove, climb up to her room, light her wood stove, and plan her teaching for the next day. The primary-reading grids and the exercise books of the youngest children would keep her up till midnight, her only company the strikes from the clock, every half hour.

The next day, it would start all over. At times, she would feel ground down, but she held drawing sessions, during which the children, even she, would be taken in by the study of details. Peace and quiet would return, for a few moments. When chaos came back, she turned the situation around by having the pupils listen for silence, the only sound a fly here, or a bird there.

Once the subjects were covered and teaching was over for the day, once the dishes were done and put away, it has to be said, loneliness was back, settling in cosily, as if trying to befriend and tame Micheline. In the quiet of the night, in the heart of the Blaye countryside, dwarfed by a sky speckled with the same, familiar stars, a quote from Pascal might come back to her: "The eternal silence of these infinite spaces frightens me." She was comforted by this great Christian philosopher, knowing she was not the only one to feel apprehension, but it did not bring her closer to other humans.

When this happened, Micheline would hold on as best she could, relying on her faith to help her. On Thursdays, when there were no classes, she would go down to Le Pontet and catch the train to Blaye, then connect to Bordeaux to do some errands and join up with acquaintances from teachers' college. She found warm, adult companionship in other Catholic teachers, who organized lectures and symposia. Afterwards, they would all go to mass in a cathedral. It felt good to be among people of her own age, who shared her values. She could feel her faith evolve and grow, most particularly when attending mass with thousands of participants like herself.

*

These sweet moments of letting go are here … wrapping her up. Faith—there is nothing like faith! She relaxes. Peace … at last.

*   *

3

Often, at night, Madame Hébert's thoughts drift from one scene to another, without much connection, years apart. But now that she invited me to write her memoirs, she is beginning to put some order in her mind, straining to bring some scenes into focus. In the afternoon, when she is supposed to be resting, she cannot let go of this mental work, thinking about the implications of my arrival. My father and her late husband were childhood friends. When I looked her up two years ago, and stopped by for a visit, she began to tell me her story. We concluded, somewhat quickly, that she had a message to pass on to future generations. Now that I will be listening to her story in detail, she has to remember accurately. Also, as an afterthought, Madame Hébert wonders whether I—or anyone—shall be up to the task to convey her feelings properly.

Today, the time has come to plan for an assortment of frozen meals for my visits. Madame Hébert takes control of her homecare worker and leaves nothing to chance. The order is placed by phone with the supermarket and will be delivered within the week. By the time the homecare worker has washed, ironed, folded, and put away the last load of laundry, Madame Hébert does not feel like eating lunch. Supervising is tiresome, but eat she must, in order to take the pill the doctor ordered. So, she swallows the pill—with an indefinable, distant look in her eyes.

Afternoons mean rest. The homecare worker has left and Madame Hébert walks carefully, step-by-step, to settle into her armchair. TV is what she needs now. There are no National Assembly debates today, so she flits from one channel to another, as giraffes, snow-topped mountains, and soap operas parade by. Oh, soap operas, intricate plots, betrayals ... scenes get into a muddle within minutes—what do these actors know of betrayal? ...

1937 ... Easter.... The train to Paris ... The Paris of the Popular Front, two months before the opening of the International Exposition ... A group of people like her, Catholics in their twenties, going to attend symposia.... The men stayed at one hotel and the women were put in another hotel, next door. They would have breakfast together, attend lectures and mass, and visit monuments and museums, including the newly renovated Louvre.... The women were constantly swarming around one of the teachers ... he was like a magnet: "Jean" here, "Jean" there—tall, charming, well-read— his name was everywhere. All hustling to get into group photos! ... What a whirlwind! ... And later, what betrayal! ...

After Micheline was back at work in the little schoolhouse in Eyrans, she received her batch of photos from the leader, just like everyone else. Except for one line with it, inviting her to meet up with him. Yes, it was he, Jean! ... They had their first date on May Day at Bourg-sur-Gironde, south of Eyrans, halfway between Blaye and Bordeaux.

Madame Hébert can still visualize that Friday afternoon. It was sunny. She does not remember what Jean looked like, but it was the flow of his speech that drew her in. They had strolled through the little streets, and up and down the esplanade, contemplating the confluence of the Dordogne and Garonne Rivers. They pursued their exploration down to the port, outside the fortifications. Sitting side-by-side on the grass, by the muddy waters, they could only guess at the damages caused by the record high tide only weeks before.

They spent some time in silence. Then Jean leaned toward Micheline, and she turned away. Jean's move changed the mood like a punch. There had been a misunderstanding. Something was missing for Micheline, Jean was rushing. They both clammed up and returned to Blaye by coach, to catch separate trains home. "See you again...."

"... See you again."

Although these words were spoken mechanically, it committed them to seeing each other again, and soon thereafter they were meeting. This time they were able to speak more easily and their meetings transformed into long talks. They discovered each other by way of literature, beating around the bush and politely avoiding personal matters. Jean came across as somewhat too clever in his compliments: "Micheline, you are like a fountain of fresh water." And he liked her 'natural candour'. She was unaccustomed to this kind of expressiveness and did not know how to respond. The words sounded sincere and touched her, but she felt she was operating on another plane. Soon Jean's fervour resurfaced—his patience was coming to an end. He knew Micheline had idealized him from the very start. Quoting Mauriac's latest novels, he tried to convince her that romanticism was only an illusion. Micheline took up reading Mauriac, hoping that would put an end to Jean's sweet nothings. She spent all her free time, at night before going to sleep, and on weekends, with a book by Mauriac in her hands. Unfortunately for her and Jean, Micheline lost interest in this writer. She drifted away from Jean to the point that their discussions turned into heated debates. And, as he was developing his answer to the simple question, "Is love possible without respect?" Jean revealed he was having an affair with a married woman. This confession struck Micheline like a shower of ice water. All of a sudden, her reference points had vanished and she could not tell where she stood or what she stood for. From then on, she felt a new realization starting to crystallize in her. Just as it had been for her parents, life had to be sustained by the kind of love that led to marriage and children. The rest—schemes, emotional impulses—belonged to the classical theatre and tragedies, and she certainly could not relate to them. The get-togethers between Micheline and Jean simply petered out. She took it as a personal failure that affected her for a long time: the word 'setback' still looms in her mind.

The following summer, while she was still not fully recovered from her pain over Jean, Micheline suffered another emotional upset. It began almost in the same way, but this time there were fireworks, and a fireball ending.

For several years, Micheline had spent part of her summer holidays with her parents north of Étauliers, on the outskirts of Royan, at Saint-Palais-sur-Mer, in a pinewood a hundred metres from the beach, at the cottage built by her father and a mason. She would visit Gilberte, her old schoolmate from teachers' college, who took her holidays in Royan with her parents and her brother, Guillaume. They would invite each other to their parents' places, and they were like brothers and sisters. Over the years, Micheline had opportunities to exchange ideas with Guillaume and she noticed, as her parents had pointed out, that he was rather loose in matters of faith and spirituality. She decided on her own to be on her guard, but at some point her parents began meddling. Once, she was so exasperated that she stormed out of the room, slamming the door.

In that particular summer, as they watched what probably were the 1938 Bastille Day fireworks, Guillaume, now a strong and healthy air-force conscript, took her hand in the darkness. She remained perfectly motionless and heard him whisper, "Gotcha!" Although she did not feel attracted to him, she did not pull her hand away, and a somewhat belated sense of guilt descended upon her.

"You are not to see him again!" she thought to herself, the following day, as she watched him go back to his base. Where could this idea have come from? By now, the world seemed bogged down in an international imbroglio; just about everywhere there were talks of general and partial mobilizations, especially since the Sudeten crisis and Italy's designs on Tunisia, but all this fuss must have come from just a few opinion makers. Micheline's thought of not seeing Guillaume again had nothing to do with him being an airman.

The fact remains that Guillaume soon wrote her a letter, and at the end of it he asked for a lock of her hair. Micheline's reply was short and unequivocal: she did not share his feelings and as far as she was concerned, she was through with him. A while later, however, she received a letter from Gilberte that started like this—she remembers the words, only too well: "For eight days, now, I have been without a brother...." Guillaume's bomber had crashed in Algeria. Micheline was struck with horror, haunted to this day, with recurring pictures of explosions and flames engulfing Guillaume: "Oh my...."

*

Madame Hébert looks away and sighs.

So many things to settle.... All these characters popping up from time to time.... So much weight ... such a burden.

And now, what about this young man, me, this new ghostwriter, will he be able to grasp all this? And what if he ends up twisting the meaning she wants to give to her memories? ...

The TV plays on while Madame Hébert is in the midst of her siesta....

* *

4

When I stand at her door, Madame Hébert steps back with her head tilted slightly to one side, giving me an impression of shyness, despite her age. Generally speaking, she has not changed since I last saw her two years ago. I figure she must have plenty of pluck to have me, a near stranger—even if she knew my parents—take on anew what failed to transpire in her first memoirs. If Madame Hébert chose me, it must be because her husband's grandchildren, Laure, Yann, and Gildas, do not have the time to record her life. Or perhaps she does not want to compromise their relationship with her, for while they are aware of some of the twists and turns of her life, she was, at least at the beginning, the 'other woman' in their mother's eyes. And if I accepted, it is because her selection of memories, or rather, what she lingered over in our first discussions, deeply puzzled me. What in essence makes her choose one memory over another? This still escapes me but, at this stage, I leave it aside.

If we follow Madame Hébert's story in sequence, it comes to an abrupt end, Hollywood style: she meets a wonderful man, they marry and live happily ever after. If on the other hand, the present context, namely the conclusion of Madame Hébert's life, can be recorded and analyzed in the light of past events, and past events reviewed in the light of the present, the scale of values that made her life worth living

27

becomes blurred. On those terms, while exploring the question of personal freedom, we decided her modest story might convey a painful lesson of tolerance and relativity. Naturally, this realization did not come to me immediately.

The first days of her narrative have no sequence; I let Madame Hébert jump from one event to another. This way, I can gauge the importance of each one in her memory. But then, blanks need to be filled in when reviewing everything, and I am faced with the slight problem that she refrains from giving me the names of all the people in her story. But I sense I must not insist.

Thus, on this first morning, we agree on the details of our meetings. One of them is that she does not want her voice to be recorded. I shall arrive in the morning, take notes in writing, have lunch with her, and then leave in the afternoon to rewrite a first draft of her statements. The next day, before resuming, we shall review my notes from the previous day. On the whole, I will be a post-fact observer, and objective, inasmuch as I am aware of the 'Copenhagen Interpretation', according to which the stated result of an experiment is dependent on its observer.

Based on these parameters, I began recording what has just been related about Madame Hébert's life, from her birth until 1938.

*

And so, here we are, face-to-face in Madame Hébert's kitchen. We had left off in 1938. 1939.... That was the year her sister Marcelle married at Easter and moved out of Étauliers to Saint-Ciers-sur-Gironde, their county seat. This prompted Micheline to ask for a transfer out of Eyrans in the hope of staying close to her. Marcelle was the sister who did not believe in God.

That June, Micheline found herself delegated to another township to grade national exams, as a representative of state schools. Her colleagues felt their integrity was challenged by the legal requirement to have a private-school observer—a 'religious bigot'—monitor the national grading of private-school and state-school pupils. These colleagues were circulating a petition demanding the removal of the private-school observer. In the meantime, Micheline noticed that one of her state-school colleagues had given lower marks to pupils who wore a religious symbol. Resting her decision on the regulations in force, she refused to sign the petition. At lunchtime, she could sense a mounting tension from her colleagues, and when she returned to her desk to resume grading, she found the petition with everybody's signature except hers. And again she refused to sign.

She was summoned a short time later to the office of the district director where she was informed that her standpoint had been reported to the Bordeaux School Inspectorate and that it might jeopardize her transfer. It was only after numerous justifications had been presented, and certainly after various negotiations had occurred at different levels, that Micheline's transfer to the county seat was approved. The primary stipulation was that she was not to meet private-school staff.

She never did move to the new school. It was towards the end of that summer, while she was visiting her parents, that they received a postcard from their son, Rémy. It confirmed mobilization: France was going to war. All transfers were cancelled, and Micheline was to stay in Eyrans. She resigned herself to her destiny and, strangely, in spite of all her efforts, after giving it some thought, she felt relieved.

Micheline's brother to their parents—Paris, Mon., 28 Aug. 1939 (postcard):

Paris 28th August 1939

Dear Parents

There is no need to describe the fever that has taken over Parisians. It must be the same everywhere.

The sight of railway stations crowded with army reserves joining their units is deeply saddening.

Several of my colleagues have

E. BAUDELOT & CIE, Impr., 41, avenue Reille, Paris (XIVᵉ).

been called up. Employees like me staying with the railway will probably have to leave Paris.

I wish I had good news but we are no better informed than anywhere. We are waiting.

With love to all,

Rponthier

* *

5

The war had arrived. Cities and villages were drained of their young men. Quiet in the streets, restrictions, the unknown—a new world was creeping in. It was difficult to know what to believe from the radio. What had it been like in 1914? In any case, this time men had not gone off parading with flowers in the barrels of their guns.

People waited. Nothing happened. Time seemed to stand still.

The Ponthier family cottage by the sea, at Saint-Palais-sur-Mer, was requisitioned by the military. At school, it became impossible to avoid talking about the front. As weeks went by, winter got closer; woollens and items thought to be of comfort to soldiers were collected. When the time came to package them and ship them, Micheline added greeting cards cut out by the children, who had drawn pine trees and written a few words. December was promising to be cold and she hoped the gifts would arrive before Christmas.

And indeed, at the beginning of the following year, Micheline received two letters of thanks from an infantry lieutenant.

*

As we are having lunch face-to-face, Madame Hébert tells me a few details about the lieutenant. Then she candidly offers to show me the letters. I raise the bottle and offer her another glass of claret. After dessert, she drags me, step by step, to a kind of pantry between the garage and the vestibule that leads to the living room. This is where boxes and papers are stored. She bends over carefully and, almost without hesitation, she pulls out a shoebox, the colour a somewhat faded blue, and hands it to me. She then leads me to a bedroom that has been converted into an office, pulls up the blind, and finally lifts the cover to reveal letters and papers filling three quarters of the box.

That is where her secrets were. She had kept them there, completely rightfully, with the full assent of her gentleman of a husband. I could not help recalling how I had discarded so many letters in my life, to turn a page or start a new chapter, and I wondered if it had been a mistake. Was I less sensitive than she? Had I somehow misread her because of her reserved manner?

She mumbles a few words as she sorts some papers, and then she pulls out the postcard her brother had sent their parents from Paris in August 1939. She also hands me the lieutenant's letters. The next day she will allow me to leaf through this rather personal correspondence and to photograph it. The following days she leaves me alone. I could decide then, on my own, the relevance of the texts, while she takes her afternoon naps in the living room. That is how I ended up handling those papers right between my fingers—messages of so much hope and so many feelings from the past. There were short notes and long letters, signatures, dates, a Belgian envelope with the swastika of the German censors—it was all there from nearly seventy years ago. Could life possibly be revived where it had stopped, in a different universe?

A lieutenant to Micheline's pupils: Thanks for the gifts—Field Post, Tues., 26 Dec. 1939:

The Front 26th December 1939

Dear Children,

Children, let me tell you a story that happened to us soldiers in a place where not very many nice things are happening.

On the morning of December 24, a few kilometres at the rear, I was told: "There are Christmas parcels for your battalion, take them along." Christmas parcels—of course I would take them along. I started counting them, feeling them through their cloth and paper wrappings, and guessing at the kind of surprises hidden in them. They were somewhat soiled from their long journey, but still quite tempting, I must say. I had them loaded up, and away we went to our mates.

Ah, those mates are quite far from you, my friends! They are over there, in the middle of a black forest that has turned all white and is rattling from rime. Hoarfrost is quite beautiful, you know, but it is not warm at all, especially when you have to live in the woods where, every minute, the slightest wind will poke you treacherously with thousands of tiny ice needles around the neck and ears.

Soon I arrive there, at a big forest of beech and oak trees, with the more promising parcels in my hands, the biggest of them, well wrapped and tied up, marked as: "From the Girls' School of Eyrans, Gironde." As I walk into the forest along a narrow, frozen path, I announce:

"Come on out, guys, Father Christmas is here!"

You should have seen them, those large, muffled-up guys, unshaven or with beards, coming out stiff from under their dirt shelters, and flocking up to me.

"I'll hand them out in a minute, with those from the depot!" (The depot is a small station in the middle of nowhere, where trains don't come anymore; we use it as a shed.)

And so I get down into my own shelter that is dug out underground and covered with tree trunks and clay, and

I begin sorting the parcels. A moment later, after the men have been told, I start distributing the contents. Oh, no, not to all the men, I would not have all 800 of them show up here! Imagine, the enemy is right next to us, over there, down by the edge of the woods, on the other side of the little brook, barely a few hundred metres away, and we have to watch him carefully, without revealing ourselves. This is why I have only a few men come over and collect for the others.

We spread out a large sheet of paper on the ground, and here we go. – Hey! A lighter! Everybody wants it, of course.

Good, thick socks, with a batch of crossword puzzles—what a nice idea! Another pair of socks with a card game—what a deal! A scarf, books, and still more items, on and on! I am being squashed, the men are going to choke me—do I have to get angry?

It is the same for all the parcels, as exclamations pop from all sides: –Oh! –Ah! –Look at that! –How cute! –What thoughtful children! –What kind people! On, and on, and on. I must say that more than one of these men, of these fatigued and hardened men, had to wipe a tear with the tip of their large fingers when I showed them the little cards so sweetly decorated with pine trees and rabbits. I must admit, I felt more overcome than the others, for I have not always been a soldier. I have a flashback to my own pupils, my very own boys and girls from my class in the Loire Valley, but it makes me even happier to realize that the pupils of our schools remember their soldiers who endure a harsh life, far from their families and villages.

So, children, this is what I wanted to tell you: I wanted to tell you that your package has arrived, that it made a lot of us happy, and above all, I wanted to thank you.

I am sending you a big thank you from all of us, as we feel so lucky and spoiled. The men are poorly equipped and so tired right now, they probably will not write to you—they are holed up, in trenches in the woods, facing the enemy.

Thank you for your gifts!

Thank you for your wishes and your "Happy Christmas!"

I wish I could thank each of you individually but the wrappings are now gone with the gifts.

There is one I managed to keep, so I could have at least one name: Marie Saulnier, age 10, Pontet Eyrans (Gironde). This kind little girl wrote her signature, together with that of a certain Etienne, probably her brother, also a nice boy, whom we thank for his "Happy Christmas" – Thank you again to all those whose names I do not have, and a Happy New Year to all the pupils of the School of Eyrans, to their schoolmistress, and to their families.

D***

Lieutenant A*** D*** — 151st Infantry
3rd Battalion — Postal Sector 1S3
Schoolmaster at **** (****)

The lieutenant to Micheline: Thanks for the pupils' gifts—Field Post, Tues., 26 Dec. 1939:

The Front 26 December 1939

Dear Miss Ponthier,

I am writing to you to acknowledge receipt of a parcel, sent by you and your pupils, that has reached us on the front in Alsace-Lorraine. I am the officer who collected it and divided it. It happens that I am also a schoolmaster and I wish to express to you how I was personally touched by your generous parcel, more as a schoolmaster than as a soldier. You must know how much everything concerning education can touch us.

I am thanking you in the name of all the men you spoiled! Thank you especially for the books. I have not distributed them yet: danger is rampant, breaks are few, and cold is everywhere—this is not the time for reading, but we will soon get some relief, and that is when the books will be appreciated. They will help chase away boredom and, above all, help us think a little, for it is not easy on the frontline, where only material needs and preservation of life count.

I can assure you in all sincerity, that all I am writing your pupils is true, and that our men have been overwhelmed and deeply moved indeed, resembling big children who rejoice at any sign of sympathy or generosity.

You see, it is not material things we miss the most, although it feels difficult to many. It is fairly easy to switch to the rough life, to get used to eating anything, any time, and sleeping anywhere with all our clothes on. The hard part is to be away from one's own kind, far from friends and far from all that makes life real and moral. This is why we appreciate not only gifts but also, even more so, the thoughts that come with them.

In the name of all the recipients, thank you again to you and your pupils.

With gratitude, yours faithfully,

D***
Lieutenant D*** in the field
151ˢᵗ Infantry
3ʳᵈ Battalion Postal Sector 163
In better days: schoolmaster at **** (****)

Micheline wrote back immediately to the lieutenant; he was a schoolmaster in civilian life. Soon, on a snowy, icy day, she received an answer, marking the beginning of an on-going correspondence, that included more parcel shipments, and during which the lieutenant was reassessing his life after ten years of marriage. They discussed values, human nature, and peace—until April 25, 1940. That was the last time the lieutenant wrote her, for two weeks later, the Germans went on the offensive.

The lieutenant to Micheline: An appreciation of her vision—Field
Post, Sun., 21 Jan. 1940:

The Front 21ˢᵗ January

Dear Miss Ponthier,

*Yorour letter reached me, or rather, was waiting for me on
my return from leave. I was back with a heavy heart, back
from twelve days of family bliss—with the date to report back
ever closer in my mind. I had just left my wife, my 5-year-old
son, and a fat 4-month old baby who was just beginning to
recognize me and to give me pretty smiles. Surely you
understand how breaking all connections with a former life,
leaving behind one's environment and the nest built over
years of labour and love, and abandoning all those who
breathe life into it, tears one apart. That is precisely the state
of mind I was in, after a hard journey with endless trials up to
the frontline, when I found your letter waiting. Well, I can
assure you that I found solace in it and I shall tell you why.
(Now, it is not my wish to sound ridiculous but if I do, I beg
for leniency.)*

*Your letter moved me because it brought me back to a time
when I used to believe in quite a few things, like Justice and
the goodness of men—see, I am starting to be foolish—I was
only 22 or 23. My wife was even more enthusiastic about high
ideals; while I had moments of doubt, she <u>believed</u>—and was
so confident, so candid, so generous!*

*p. 2) In the past eight years she has changed so much - -.
Moving from one disappointment to the next, since last
September's setback, all her nice confidence has run out, and
she there seems to be no other way. I am the only one left
standing with courage and hope this time, the one at the
forefront of the fight—and, oh, what a brawl!*

*Not that there is much real danger, we spend more time
being on the look-out than fighting. What is more depressing
than those villages, deserted and silent; those houses with
overturned, empty furniture; those lifeless gardens; this snow
that keeps falling; these villages and streets and gardens,*

where children can only be called to mind by shredded toys scattered all around; and indoors, beds and cradles lying overturned, ripped open, and trampled down. – How can you hang on to hope after all this – . – And so, we become mean and hateful – inasmuch as we feel that those at the rear have made themselves cosily at home in this war, at least those who are unscathed by it – . So you can understand how your letter, inspired as it was by a generous and delicate soul, was like a ray of sunshine for me in the middle of a storm $=$ (really, my writing is awkward! How clumsy can a man be in expressing his thoughts.

You could be like so many, ignoring us and merely dealing with your own troubles and hardships! But here you are, coming to join us, thinking about us, sharing with our hardships.

There is a sentence I liked especially: "to prepare for an after-the-war that will be worthy of our sacrifices." Oh, how much I wish that, for all these young men,
p. 3) disillusioned as they are to have believed, all these men who will return embittered and faithless—how much do I wish indeed for scores of Micheline Ponthiers to be found all across France to lay the groundwork for this 'after' to be hoped for, and to provide them with strength and taste for life and work

This is why I wanted to thank you

Because you helped me remember a happier time in my life, because you are not selfish, because in spite of the turmoil, you still believe in the future And rightly so, the future must be believed in, you are completely right. After disaster and death, life will be reborn. I think all this chit-chat might annoy you and I apologize for it. We ~~much~~ quite often find reasons here to grumble and curse, and I did not want to miss the opportunity to convey my appreciation to someone who deserves it (I am not the boastful kind, and neither do I share my private thoughts with just anyone)

D***

With the horrors of the Great War as a reference, it became clear this was not 1914. Worse, memories of massacres in occupied territories suddenly resurfaced. Urbanites and farmers, be they Jews, Catholics, or Protestants, took the same decision, to move south, as one people, forming an exodus—on foot and bicycles, in ox carts, trains, and automobiles, all fleeing south with their suitcases, chests of drawers, silver, mattresses, and birdcages—and blocking the French army on roadways. Dishevelled, dirty, and breathing heavily, they wondered where their air force was, when they emerged from ditches, after being strafed from the air.

Soon a stream of Belgian and French cars began rolling through Le Pontet—Medusa rafts trying to squeeze their way, day after day, onto the only bridge to Bordeaux. Within a month of this debacle, Bordeaux's population tripled; supplying it with bread was a nightmare, and Spanish and Basque refugees were moved to camps in the outlying areas. The harbour and the estuary were jammed with over one hundred and fifty ships flying different national flags, waiting to evacuate bona fide refugees. New radio frequencies announced an imminent Communist coup in Paris.

As May 1940 was ending, the situation was becoming more and more tense, but the teaching body was ordered to stay in place. In Étauliers, where close to two hundred and fifty Belgians of all ages had been accommodated by the locals, Monsieur Ponthier, who was always thinking ahead, removed the wheels from his Renault Celta 4. At night in Le Pontet, at the crossroads between Bordeaux and Blaye, still more southbound refugees, with their vehicle lights off, would stop at Monsieur Iroz's country inn and ask whether there were any rooms left. Micheline met a young schoolmistress from Brussels, towing in her wake a dozen Flemish-speaking children whose parents were already billeted in the village. She quickly made arrangements with her colleague, who also served as municipal clerk, for the children to use the school.

At a certain point—it must have been around June 17, 1940—there was talk of an armistice, and the flow of refugees petered out. Everything stopped and silence took over, as if people were holding their breath. Some thought it was too early for an armistice.

Then, barely a week later, a hum never heard before began to grow and overtake the countryside. Micheline was heading to her parents' in Étauliers, and she saw it coming towards her, in the direction of Blaye and its harbour, developing into an ever increasing metallic rattle with all kinds of vehicles, an endless motorized column of motorcyclists, tanks, and lorries: the first Germans. They motioned her to get off the road, into the ditch.

Into the ditch

When she arrived at her parents', she found a local Frenchwoman in German uniform requisitioning bedrooms for the local *Kommandantur*, their new neighbour who had picked the mansion, with manicured grounds across the brook, as headquarters. A few days later, when Micheline returned, she found herself in the kitchen face-to-face with two strangers in uniform, polishing their boots. The armistice had been signed and the Germans were settling in.

The Occupation had begun. The French feigned total indifference. The refugees, including the Belgians, returned home using petrol vouchers. Eleven months later, Micheline would receive a most touching letter of thanks from the young schoolmistress, written in her best French and posted from Vilvoorde, a suburb of Brussels. She had found her father's house 'untouched'.

Not a single shot had been heard. People were overwhelmed with feelings of confusion, especially since both the establishment and demagogues who had preceded all these complications had vanished into thin air. Now, the only thing left was to believe that 'armistice' meant 'peace'.

*

A so-called 'official time' was put in place by Radio-Paris, and clocks in town halls and train stations in the occupied zone were moved forward by an hour to harmonize with the central European time of Berlin. Mail deliveries resumed, but Micheline received no more letters from the lieutenant. Various directives coming from different *Kommandanturen* were broadcast by loud-speakers mounted on vehicles, by town criers, by the press, or on bilingual posters with French as the second language, and invariably ending with death threats. Guns, rifles, pistols, and revolvers by the hundreds, along with their ammunition, were laid down obediently at town halls; sabres were also surrendered. Carrier pigeons were ordered destroyed. The first executions following acts of sabotage started in July. In Étauliers, life returned to normal very slowly, to a new kind of normalcy, interspersed with curfews and night patrols.

Micheline needed to see a dentist. She managed to travel to Bordeaux and cross the bridge, now under German guard.

While staying a couple of nights with her former guardians from teachers' college, she learned that at the end of the German thrust, about a week before the armistice, nine schools (including the trade school on Cours de la Marne, in the vicinity of the main railway station) had been shelled and some sixty were dead. August marked the beginning of the RAF bombardments of the Bec d'Ambès refinery and the Trompeloup train station, south and west of Eyrans. Two months later, Bordeaux was bombed. Its citizens were submitted to scores of false alarms, always at night. During the first year of the Occupation, Bordeaux had an average of two bombardments or false alarms per month.

* *

6

I can't quite remember which day of our interviews it was, but on that particular morning, as I rang the bell after having walked through the little gate without noticing the number of vehicles parked on the street, a woman who was still young-looking appeared at the door, flanked by a slightly younger man. I recognized her right away. "Ah, Monsieur! ..." she said in one breath, making me wonder why she called me 'Monsieur'. She had pronounced it so exquisitely, with her arms stretching towards me and grasping my hands from underneath, as if to support them, in a move both soft and temperate. I had never been welcomed in such a way in my life, and I rested my gaze on her eyes as I felt her thumbs folding over. I gathered that this was a solemn moment, and now I wondered whether the 'Monsieur' had been a way of counterbalancing her familiarity towards me, in front of the young man. Then again, she might not have recognized me. In an instant, my memory was flooded with flashbacks. I had seen her life unfold, decade after decade, in Madame Hébert's photo albums: vacations, her wedding, baptisms. She almost resembled my mother, with a rounder face, which added to my confusion. I had been introduced to her forty-nine years earlier, never to meet again—until that morning. It was she, Laure, as I had remembered her in her grey school skirt, at what was going to be my last *slava* celebration with my parents. Following this "Ah, Monsieur!..."

she continued, trying to suppress her emotions, "My brother Yann is dead." Then she bowed her head and let go my hands.

I was struck by her composure and wondered whether she owed it to her Catholic education or to medical tribulations she had endured; this might have given her a certain resilience. She looked somewhat pale, her features were in relative proportion to one another, but in spite of her calmness, one could sense a slight uneasiness. I also had to reconsider the young man standing beside her; he looked so much like Yann himself that I had to make an effort to realize that it was his father who had died.

Here I was, hearing the announcement of a death, in a Bordeaux suburb, by a sister and a son, and the deceased was not Madame Hébert, and the nephew was not the brother, and the son was not his father. But Bordeaux was my Bordeaux— and suddenly I was a little boy again, I was a son, watching my mother in a state of shock, gliding by me in slow motion, without seeing me, floating as if levitating towards her own mother, to tell her of the death of her husband—my father— leaving me alone, to lean against the wall. And a month later, in the middle of the night, it was my turn to be given the same news in person: "Well, my child, here it is, your mother has had an accident...."

Now, in spite of myself, after so many years, I was just as devastated, wondering why I was being put through this once more, after having made my peace with the past—I, a stranger from a distant land, having to reveal this weakness of mine. My face contorted, tears welled up in my eyes, I had no choice but to turn my back on Laure and her nephew. I was incapacitated by images of my own uprooted youth, incapable of sharing in their mourning—betraying the very course I had accepted as my own, as a free man.

For what seemed like the longest time, I questioned the tops of the trees and the wind moving the clouds, while Laure stood in silence behind me. I wondered whether I should give her an explanation, but not now. I told myself that I would have to muster the strength at another time.

The house was still dark inside, a few shapes circling around a dishevelled Madame Hébert who was barely able to pronounce my name when she saw me. She had outlived her fifty-eight-year-old grandson, the one who had supported her through a very difficult time in her life. The self-assurance of the words she had used when recounting her life to me was now swept away by her sensitivity. Yann's children were there, busy with their telephones, and the new love of his life moved aimlessly around the dining room, alone, looking through images of him spread out on the table. I whispered my sympathy to each and every one, and as I took my leave, Madame Hébert and I agreed on our next appointment. I felt much obliged that I was not expected to attend the funeral.

*

I went to the industrial district of La Bastide to be alone. I needed to reconnect with a past I had neglected. In spite of the path I had chosen, I realized my past was the most personal thing that belonged to me, regardless of what life had in store for me—in fact, one's past is far beyond a question of possession, it is a state of being.

There was a tang in the air as I halted on a bridge to light a cigarette with my back turned to the wind. I rested my elbows on the edge of the bridge, over a rail yard, and proceeded to observe the abandoned warehouses and tracks of the old La Bastide railway station. As a child, I had spent countless hours perched on the back of an armchair, studying them, trying to predict the comings and goings of tractors and carriages. I had to tame my childhood again, just as Madame Hébert was taming her youth, with my assistance, but it was through her—and through the death of her grandson— that I found myself, completely by surprise, transposed into my

distant past. She and I were still unaware of what subtle effects
an unexpected death can have on memories.

At the other end of the bridge I could see the street
where my mother would take me along in a pushchair,* between
workmen's garden plots and charred hangars. Now, new
warehouses lined the street, and a dog barked angrily as I
strolled by. The emptiness of the street offered me the same
quiet and protective solitude of my boarding-school years in
eastern France, when I was let out Sunday afternoons and
watched air-force cadets roaming deserted streets in groups of
two. At the end of the street lay the Garonne River, where my
mother's stroll ended, and we would sit on the embankment and
look at remnants of shipwrecks from the war years. I thought I
might still see them there.

* *

---

* North American English: stroller.

7

Children went back to school in September of 1940, under reformed rules that started to be introduced under the new order. Resignation became the modus vivendi for many people, including Micheline's parents in Étauliers. The two Germans used the kitchen to do their own cooking and, like any forty-year-old farmers, they were found to be as "correct and respectful" as they could be. They were heard sometimes discussing hardware items in her father's shop. Communicating with them could not take place until Micheline, who knew a few words of German, visited her parents. During one such interaction they learned that a French POW worked on one of the Germans' farm, in Bavaria. Then, little by little, it was discovered that this Frenchman was a native of the nearby Department of Charente. The Bavarian proposed to relay news between the prisoner and his family. A meeting was arranged between the French wife and the Bavarian. He did manage to have a letter and cognac safely delivered to her husband. Soon thereafter, however, the two Germans were transferred, singing *Es war ein Edelweiss* as they left, without ever being heard from again. They were replaced by a younger German.

This new tenant was a former student who found his army food vile. He, too, got in the habit of cooking his meals in the Ponthiers' kitchen and, with the few French words he knew, he could communicate much more easily than his two comrades had. This came in handy, as he was an amateur photographer. It was around this time, during All-Saints holidays, that Micheline discovered some clothes that had belonged to her grandmother, in the attic, and tried them on. When she made her appearance in the kitchen, the German dropped his potatoes for his camera and requested that Micheline pose for him.

Photo: anonymous, copy by J. L. F. Lambert, courtesy of M. H***

Micheline photographed by the German soldier
Étauliers, 1940

Once they were outside in the garden she changed her mind, but the German insisted and won his case, only to have Micheline demand that he surrender both the photos and the negatives.

This young German stayed at the Ponthiers' only a few months, and there were no more tenants after him. Only later people realized, after the Balkans had been invaded, that Germany had redeployed her armies.

Generally speaking, Germans were never addressed in public. The French grew to distrust them because of ever-increasing requisitions and bans. Some people spied on one another, even within families. Businessmen profited from the sudden devaluation of the franc, at least at the onset; they became used to their new German customers and eventually called them by name.

In Étauliers, during mass, one German would come and stand alone by a pillar, behind the worshippers, and listen to Micheline's oldest sister play the harmonium. Because he was an organist and found it so compelling, he asked for permission to play when mass was not being held. Soon, it became usual to hear sounds of baroque and romantic music in the middle of the week, coming from within the walls of the church.

And little by little, rumours started spreading about all sorts of things, including relationships between one or two young laundresses and servicemen from the occupying forces.

*

Gossip and anecdotes were no substitute for a full life. Back in Eyrans, isolation was growing heavier, more oppressive. Once again, the emptiness Micheline had felt as a young girl at catechism was catching up with her, and one way or another, she would continue with her struggle. Around this time, Micheline was scheduled to have her nasal septum operated on in Bordeaux and she was entangled in red tape while searching for a substitute teacher. A letter from an old schoolmate, dated March 1941, gives a picture of her situation. Her friend ascribes Micheline's malaise to lukewarm faith; as a believer, the answer would be to pull oneself together and strengthen one's faith: "Don't say, 'He's leaving me to my little, mediocre life'. ... Christ is telling you, 'Come'; He is calling you, and He is waiting for you."

The operation was performed in May under local anaesthetic, by a discharged army doctor. The following night, Micheline barely survived a haemorrhage, which lengthened her recovery by several days. She could not be moved, and one night, at the sound of an air-raid siren, she was left in her bed when everyone else took to the shelters. Her convalescence continued in Bordeaux, at the home of her college guardians, and then in Eyrans. She finally resumed teaching before summer arrived. That day, her colleague recommended she have lunch at Monsieur Iroz's country inn, down in Le Pontet, and she decided to allow herself this. And indeed, the place turned out to be quite warm and pleasant.

***

PART II

8

When school started again in September of 1941, Micheline decided to return to Iroz's, where Basque cooking was still served in spite of food shortages. The restaurant became popular with the Germans but the French regular patrons kept seating at their usual long table, all together. One such customer was the new doctor, replacing the general practitioner who had recently retired. This newcomer was tall and slender and kept to himself. Micheline learned from the villagers that he was thirty-one; a native of the Charente Department; and had been repatriated from a rural post in the Levant. He was a Protestant, the son of a minister, and was not married. His name was Jacques Celse.

"Excuse me…. Could you please pass me the decanter?" That is how Micheline addressed the doctor the first time; she was thirsty.

They encountered each other again and again, day after day, at the regulars' table and began to speak more often, about their respective occupations.

When was it that Monsieur Iroz set them at a separate table? Was it following the mass execution of hostages from Nantes and Bordeaux, reported in the press? Madame Hébert does not remember. Perhaps it was to put them slightly further away from those "gentlemen," but in any case, it was less noisy. However, one day, a German walked over to her as she was waiting for the doctor, and asked her if she would care to sit with him in the company of his colleagues. It was a wasted attempt.

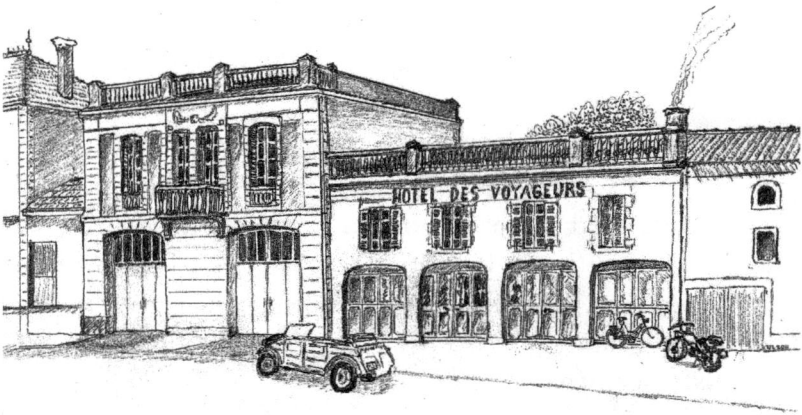

Monsieur Iroz's country inn, Le Pontet

*

When I ask her to describe the doctor for me, Madame Hébert widens her eyes, she purses her lips, and she declares that she is incapable of doing so, just like for all the characters in her story. Whether it is the colour of his eyes, the shape of his chin, or anything at all, I cannot extract anything from her.

Later, when I renew my attempt, she interjects: "But you already asked me that!"

"… But … how about spectacles?" Nothing comes to her. I prompt her again: "How about cigarettes?"

"… Perhaps … from time to time …"

As for their inspiration or attraction, or might I say 'interest', it was clear that they shared common ground. Each was thirsty for knowledge, curious about life and its mysteries.

Yet both had a need for human relations and a regard for others. Finally, it surfaces that the doctor's hair was straight, dark, and brushed back.

*

And so ended 1941 for Micheline, wrapped up with the teaching routine, a few visits to her parents' home in Étauliers, and a string of lunches taken at Iroz's inn with the doctor. As Christmas approached, Micheline and her pupils put on a short skit, in which the children sang and played a doctor and his patients. She became sick the day before the performance, but the doctor managed to put her back on her feet for a few hours, long enough for the play to be enacted on time, in the classroom, in front of the parents. Upon leaving her sick bed, on her way to the show, Micheline discovered a mysterious bunch of violets on her kitchen buffet.

*

The winter of 1942 was particularly severe. Micheline had not quite recovered from her cold in January when she had to go on a physical training course in a Bordeaux suburb. It ended up being four weeks of training on a mud-filled obstacle course, interspersed with game activities. The rhythm of daily trips in and out of downtown, where she slept at night during the curfews, left Micheline totally exhausted.

In those days, the health of the teaching staff was managed free of charge by the township doctor. When Micheline returned to Eyrans and resumed going to the village restaurant in February, the doctor inquired about her recovery. She admitted that she had been severely tested by the programme; however, she went on to describe the activities she had learned to organize, and declared she was planning a project for her pupils, possibly in time for Easter.

Based on her experience of the skit staged at Christmas, Micheline could now see more broadly; she could imagine producing a play of more interest to the parents and—"Why not?"—use the returns to pay for her teaching supplies. A play with music would do the trick. She would stage *Sleeping Beauty*.

*

"Pardon me?!" Did I hear correctly? I ask her to confirm, but she continues, making no reference to the symbolism of the title, no reference to a potential political reprimand, ruled by her memories, just as my youth overwhelmed me when Yann died, blocking out the present. And that is how it will be each time. I realize that, consciously or not, whether we want it or not, we are both under the influence of our respective pasts. Madame Hébert stays on track and does not offer many metaphors either; she is straightforward—metaphors belong to literature.

*

The production of *Sleeping Beauty* caught on. After convincing her colleague to let his pupils join the cast, the number of actors and extras rose to sixty. Micheline was also given the use of Monsieur Iroz's coach garage as theatre space, for free. It was as if nothing could stop her. The following weeks were quite intense for her and I think that, as she opens her memories to me, she would have appreciated some words of encouragement, no matter how small, from the doctor.

Once the roles were cast, rehearsals had to be coordinated. The girls were to sing at recess and practice dance after class; the boys would join in after their Sunday football game, on the stage that had been set up in the garage. Soon the whole township was fired up with the project, and mothers were endlessly discussing the set and costumes.

At lunchtime, Micheline and the doctor shared issues concerning the children and their families' health problems. As a result, they agreed to re-allocate some National Relief assistance, of which Micheline was the local coordinator. United in an act of Christian charity, a Catholic and a Protestant worked together for the relief of their neighbours.

The doctor finally joined the theatre production team—on Easter Eve—wearing a pull-over and no tie. He hung the curtains and became the stagehand for the show. The performance was held the following night in the makeshift hall packed with over four hundred people who had come on foot or by bicycle from the whole region. The recital was a whirlwind of songs and dances performed in tutus, muslin dresses and hennins, accompanied by the mayor's wife at the piano. It ended with the tune of *Maréchal, nous voilà!*

The revelling stretched well past midnight. Micheline was exhausted. The doctor walked her home, up the hill, to the school. He waited for her to climb the stairs ... and walked away.

*

Madame Hébert raises her arms high: "A di-sas-ter!"

Dare I understand her correctly?

"That was the last straw!" She appears about to fly into a passion. I try to stay focussed. She explains simply: "I was at my breaking point. I burst into tears. I took the next day off."

Each time we went over this section, Madame Hébert would repeat, word for word, "Look here! It's a disaster!"—as if this were enough information for me to understand. However, I refused to interpret her mind; I had not come there to make assumptions—she had to connect the dots herself.

"Well," she offers after a moment, "the doctor does not declare his affections...."

So this was it, this is where she had been leading me for the past few days, in that prim language of her era. The doctor's silence had annoyed her: he was supposed to understand her feelings and expectations. Now, sixty-seven years later, this is still how she sees it, with such intense emotion that I am left puzzled. How could she have imagined that the doctor would actually avow his feelings for her—if he had any—simply because of what she had just accomplished—especially in light of the fact that neither of them had ever mentioned the violets he had left on her kitchen buffet four months earlier? Would it not have been more appropriate for her to expect a word of acknowledgment or respect from him—if he was indeed the source of her inspiration?

Certainly, apart from the violets, I must be missing details that Madame Hébert will not or cannot transmit to me, so deeply are they buried in her being. I decide not to interrupt her.

After all this, would it be possible she was right? Where was all this leading? Schoolchildren, their families, the township, passion for religion—were these the only things to be shared between the two of them? Clearly, the doctor had been holding back; he must have developed a keen sense of correctness. Micheline had encountered his reserve again and again. She was now trying to gauge to what extent his non-commitment went. She perceived it as a restraint, rooted in the general practitioner's personality. During their lunchtime conversations, she would probe his detachment, which was infused with a calm, steady glance, a kind of holy aloofness found amongst people who have known the desert. She sensed a deep, quiet strength that was foreign to her.

*

When she resumed teaching, after a day of recuperation, she was not feeling any better. At lunchtime, however, the doctor walked into the restaurant wearing a broad smile. He presented Micheline with the show's takings, which far exceeded all expectations. Now Micheline was able to purchase a small, electric-powered harmonium and teaching supplies. She had more plans to augment this new purchasing power, by organizing a sale of her pupils' drawings and watercolours in the restaurant.

The doctor had somehow changed, she could sense it—had he perhaps noticed something in her? He began to bring her roses that he had received from his patients. This became almost a ritual as the weeks went by, Micheline returning to the school after lunch with a box of roses attached to the back of her bicycle. When the electric harmonium arrived, he carried it on his shoulder up the hill to the school, as if he were a knight in service. And when the summer holidays finally arrived, he offered her a basket full of cherries.

*

Micheline had now returned to her parents' home, in Étauliers. It was at the beginning of that summer in 1942 when a lady who assisted the priest before mass convinced Micheline to come and help her. This devout widow had introduced Micheline's sister to the German organ player at the church. She had known Micheline since childhood, and now shared bits of gossip with her from time to time, such as how the laundresses in town carried on with the Germans. She and Micheline were to bring her sick son home from the seminary in Pessac, outside Bordeaux. He had tuberculosis complicated by pleurisy and a failed operation. His name was Luc; he was barely eighteen and wanted to be a man of God. They picked him up at the seminary, and the three of them returned all the way to Étauliers by taxi, after clearing the German check-points at the main bridges.

Back in his bed at home, in the quiet of a small, sober room, with shutters half-pulled, the young seminarian expressed an urgent need to see the doctor. The two women were at a loss, for they knew the doctor would be doing his rounds in the next village that day. But Luc insisted, to the point of sounding as though he was about to cough his final breath. Micheline left on her bicycle to look for the doctor. She found him on his motorcycle, riding in the opposite direction. As soon as he saw her, he stopped. It was now Micheline's turn to plead. She finally convinced him to come, and they met at Luc's bedside.

The two women were on one side of the bed, and the doctor on the other. Luc could not speak. He kept peering into Micheline's eyes and into those of the doctor; he then raised his hands out to both of them. He joined their hands across the bed, holding them tight, without moving, his eyes riveted on their hands. United by a man of faith for an eternity, Micheline and the doctor scarcely dared glance at each other.

Luc passed away two days later.

For the rest of the summer, Micheline never crossed paths again with the doctor. She told me they had "no reason to see each other."

*

Madame Hébert was silent for a moment. That is all she offered me on the subject.

* *

9

And so, the summer of 1942 slowly stretched into the season of hay-making and grape-picking. When autumn came it was back to school and back to teaching. Everyone went through the same motions as before, and it was natural for Micheline and the doctor to meet again at the restaurant. The doctor brought her violets on their first encounter. They started to extend their conversations after meals, by the fireplace in an adjoining room. They never alluded to the young seminarian, nor to his actions, but they approached the subjects of religion and faith a little more often. Sitting there, by the hearth, under the pretext of discussing various matters, simply in the presence of each other, they enjoyed many moments of silence while staring into the flames and watching embers turn red. Once again it would be a harsh winter.

When visiting her parents on Sundays in Étauliers, Micheline could not help but relate her growing friendship with the doctor. Finally, her mother felt obliged to ask: "Do you really think you will talk like this until you are old folks, sitting by the fire—hmm?"

This witticism sounded like approval, or even encouragement, and Micheline let a smile pass over her lips. But if the 'hmm' part, at the end of the sentence, was meant as a challenge instead of reinforcing a weak intonation, her mother's rebuttal could be interpreted as a warning that nothing else could happen between the two of them. Micheline was supposed to know why. Her mother knew and everybody knew. Church-going Catholics understood each other; there was no need to spell it out. And the son of a minister, a doctor by profession, also had to know.

Micheline gave no reply. A wall stood between Micheline and her mother. Silence invited silence. Monsieur Ponthier, on the other hand, would leave it to the young ones; he was busy enough with his store and he acknowledged that religious matters were not his department.

Autumn days went by, the unspoken lurking in the background. Fortunately, the friendship between Micheline and the doctor was not affected and continued to grow. In the evening, after class, she would ride down the hill on her bicycle, and the doctor would walk her back to the school gate. These private moments together were the only time for feelings, even if unexpressed.

*

The weeks passed, Christmas came and went, everyone worshipped with their own, and the New Year of 1943 was upon them. Micheline saw no change in store for her. She had nothing to hope for in her relationship with the doctor; they simply continued to meet at lunchtime.

Spring appeared to be coming early that year. One day, the baker's apprentice brought a plum pie to the doctor at the restaurant as a token of appreciation for a medical service. This was about the time when one of Micheline's cousins informed her that people in the village had begun to talk about her and the doctor. To Micheline, her situation seemed like a sad contrast to the coming of spring. Every Sunday, however, she would allow herself to anticipate the coming week with a kind of hope. The fortnight she spent at her parents' at Easter felt like an eternity. When she went back to teach in Eyrans, she could barely wait to get down to Iroz's for lunch, and when she reached her table, she sat down and waited. After what felt like quite a while, Monsieur Iroz managed to get to her, telling her that he would serve her right away, as the doctor was sick, very sick in fact, and had returned to his parents' in Jarnac—he had caught pneumonia only a few days earlier.

Micheline was troubled for the rest of the day. That very same night, she wrote a note to the doctor and mailed it the following morning.

There is evidence that she had confided in a friend, as a letter addressed to her, dated April 27, sums up her situation in these terms: "Moreover, it appears that the time has come for you for a definite encounter. ... We, as Christians, are meant to suffer for the salvation of humanity!" These words from her friend may lead one to conclude that Micheline had envisaged summoning the doctor to avow his love. The last sentence seems slightly exaggerated and out of context, but one may wonder if it had not been influenced by the general situation of the times. Indeed, it was around this period—a time of rationing, of more Germans all the way to the Mediterranean, and of a daring terrorist raid in Bordeaux's harbour—that roundups and dragnets went on the increase. People talked in low voices about special trains bound for Germany, and on street walls, notices of the executions of hostages grew longer. All this was happening at the same time as a Catholic renewal in France.

On May 8, the doctor wrote back to Micheline that he had been "very touched" by her note, thanking her for her concern. He signed the letter "Jacques."

He had not forgotten her. But then there was silence.

Days went by, and Micheline prayed and waited.

The prospect of seeing the doctor again after exchanging written words plunged her into expectations of a rare frenzy. But then reason would rally, and Micheline would find faults within herself. And rightly so, for when she read the doctor's note in daytime, she found it somewhat too formal. But again, at night, she found all kinds of reasons why the doctor would have used a tone that appeared dispassionate, even when the situation should have dictated the opposite.

Every day, she hoped she would find him at Iroz's.

Finally, around mid-May, Jacques was back at Le Pontet. There he was, standing in front of her. They stepped towards each other. "Ah! Jacques!..." It was as if they had always been on familiar terms.

He was so thin, so weak, so.... With a slightly embarrassed look, he confessed how much he had missed her. Then he let loose a flow of explanations on the nature of his fondness for her, which he had been feeling for a long time. He had been apprehensive about their religious differences, but now that he understood he might not have ever seen her again, he admitted he had not voiced his feelings for fear of destroying their friendship. This was what Micheline had been wondering all along. All this eruption of feelings was enough to make a person dizzy, but at bottom of it, right at the heart, she knew they were already united in Christ.

In the days that followed, Jacques and Micheline felt transported to another world. They continued to meet at Iroz's, and then again at night in the schoolyard, at the foot of the fig tree. The villagers saw them together more often and showed no sign of disapproval. It was a time for happiness and for love.

Jacques and Micheline were now at a point where they needed long walks in the countryside. Late one sunny afternoon, they stopped along an escarpment, by a windmill that was abandoned and without sails. Vineyards and fields stretched peacefully to the horizon ... air filled their lungs to capacity ... birds chirped in a bush ... and Jacques and Micheline could sense they had found a place in the order of nature. This was a moment when time should have stood still....

The world was not as bad as it was purported to be. Jacques and Micheline began to plan for the future. Happiness was there, but they believed they had to reach for it, for they had to settle a few technicalities. Jacques would need a larger practice to increase their income so they could live together, because Micheline could not expand her work in the same way. Her role would be to assist Jacques in his profession to enhance his practice. Another concern was to find a way for their respective churches to unite them in holy matrimony. In any event, they decided to tell their parents of their decision.

Time should have stood still

* *

10

The news stunned both families. In a letter dated June 7, 1943, Jacques' mother urges him to give up the whole idea. She calls Micheline selfish and insinuates that she is a false Christian. Even though Jacques and Micheline had discovered themselves in each other, in terms of religion, the 'other' was to remain the 'other'. In her letter, Jacques' mother brings up December 1929 and alludes to the passing away of Jacques' sister—should Jacques renounce his faith, it would be like a second death in the family. She did not approach the question of religion openly: she attached a note bearing the address of the minister in charge of Bordeaux's Protestant community. It was understood to be intended for the "young woman" who should pay him a visit on Rue du Hâ.

Madame Celse to her son: A plea to reconsider—Jarnac, Mon., 7 June 1943:

Jarnac Monday 7.

My dear Jacques,

After you left last night I had to tell Papa the conversation we had in his absence. Together we considered carefully the consequences of the decision that you appear to be about to make, and we both felt extremely sad. From what you told me, couldn't the matter forcing you to leave Le Pontet be resolved without such a terrible wrench? When you first mentioned that you were considering leaving your practice, we figured quite naturally that you were moving to Jarnac, but then yesterday you told me that you are not thinking of going to Jarnac. Would you have gone if the somewhat vague project developed here had been acted on? It is a pity we came too late. But there will be other opportunities! Do wait a little before going to Bordeaux: there is no situation, no matter how complicated, that cannot be resolved! I saw you leave so sad last night that something broke in me and set me back to December 1929 when God asked us that immeasurable sacrifice that is still bleeding my heart. – I don't think you have to sacrifice yourself in that way; this young woman, if she knew what kind of sacrifice you are considering, do you think she would let you do it? She would be quite selfish! – The holidays are coming up, they are starting much earlier this year; she will go home, you won't be under her influence anymore, and you will be able to see things in a new light, calmly, and with clarity. There is no choice for me but to use vague terms in this letter. But since we talked about it, couldn't we go over this situation more clearly—would you like us to come spend a day with you? Would you like me to talk to the y. woman? Your sister-in-law is too young, but I could talk to that woman as a mother and appeal to her heart; if she is ~~tru~~ *truly a Christian, there is no way she cannot understand. If I tell you all this, it is because yesterday I felt that you were extremely unhappy and that gave me great pain. We would so much like to see you happy—and truly, you deserve it! You should not torture yourself, as you tend to do sometimes, to allow this. All we ask is to help you; be frank with us, and if you want us to move one way or another, say it, we shall do as you wish. Opportunities may have been missed because of our lack of earlier discussions. If you prefer to come back, come back; we shall be in Cognac on Sunday and back on the 5:15 train. Don't use your motorcycle if that spring hasn't been changed yet, it caused us some concern. Believe me, I am writing to you with my greatest affection. All I am asking from God with all my strength is that you be happy.*

*We'll be waiting for a word from you before deciding to
come spend a day with you – Until then, love and kisses from
your mama*

J. Celse

The note included in Madame Celse's letter:

> *Monsieur le pasteur*
> *Blanc-Milsand*
> *32, rue du Hâ*
> *Bordeaux*

Micheline's mother, for her part, now referred to Jacques as the 'heretic'. Her father, who generally kept to himself (he even slept in a separate room due to a chronic cough dating from the Great War), claimed to understand nothing: "Protestant or Catholic—what's the difference?... Anyway, we have no dowry...."

Micheline wrote to a cousin who was in a seminary in a Bordeaux suburb for advice. Waiting for his answer made the situation even more oppressive. Thus, a sort of third character, invisible but tangible, infiltrated Micheline and Jacques' evening strolls.

It was obvious that each family expected the other's offspring to convert. One night, as they stood by the fig tree in the schoolyard and considered the deadlock facing them, Jacques summed up the situation by quoting an old Arab he knew from his time in the Syrian desert. The man had told him that, as far as he was concerned, converting to another religion was a fate "worse than death." Regardless, Jacques proposed that he and Micheline move forward with their plans by going to a suburb of Saintes, to the north, to appraise a new surgery that was for sale, by a doctor's widow.

A couple of days later, Jacques and Micheline left by motorcycle at 4 a.m. to catch the Bordeaux-Saintes train at Saint-Mariens. They visited the surgery, which had a garden at the back, abutting the Charente River. The rest of the day they imagined themselves living in the neighbourhood, and returned to Eyrans later that night.

*

When I reviewed this episode with Madame Hébert a few times, I asked her to explain how she sat with her skirt on the motorcycle. She obliged, specifying she had hung on to the 'driver'. In my imagination they had returned on the train with Micheline's head on Jacques' shoulder, but since she chose a formal word, I could not help but bite my lip.

Madame Hébert added that this trip had been filled with happiness, but then doubts had started creeping in. She would have to quit teaching. It seems that, despite herself, she began to realize how emancipated she had become, capable of earning her living, and committed to her career; she would certainly have felt some apprehension envisioning herself as a medical secretary. And she still had not finished paying for her education. On top of that, her teacher's pension would be reduced and the devalued franc would leave her destitute should anything ever happen to Jacques.

It was under those circumstances that Micheline received two responses in a row from her cousin, in the space of four days. In them he quoted the doctrine of the Roman Catholic Church on marriages designated as 'mixed'. He also led her to understand that her cause was not sufficiently 'sound and critical' to allow for an exception, and he suggested that it was up to the suitor to convert to Catholicism—Jacques' soul could be saved with the help of the Blessed Virgin.

Micheline was to pray and hope.

A cousin to Micheline: The Catholic doctrine and referral to a chaplain—Pont-de-la-Maye, Sun., 20 June 1943:

Petit Séminaire 20-6-43

+

Dear Cousin

We are praying intently for you at this moment. Every evening after dinner, all seven of us go to the chapel to say ten rosaries for you. We will conclude on Thursday for Corpus Christi.

I talked about it to my director and this is the requirement for the marriage to be possible:

"The Church does not exempt one from the obligation to avoid mixing religions, except for sound and critical reasons, and provided that the non-Catholic party concede to the Catholic party the complete freedom (a) of practicing his or her religion and (b) of raising all the children in the Catholic faith, and that all these commitments be duly pledged in a written form. Furthermore, both parties must vow they will not appear before a heretic minister, unless the latter is acting as a registrar (as a mayor or his deputy) and for the purpose of obtaining civil deeds."

This is the Roman Catholic Doctrine in full. My Director further told me that you could meet Reverend Father Valette, the Catholic Students' chaplain in Bx. He saw him this morning or yesterday, I think, and he told him about you. If you want to see him, ~~make~~ ask him for an appointment by letter and mention his Reverence Mr Léglise, and he will receive you. His address is 205 Rue de StGenès Bx. He is the one who may be able to enlighten you more. But of course, this is only if you wish it. It is not my intention to have you come expressly to Bordeaux, far from that!

We took the General Certificate Exam on Wednesday and Thursday. It was rather difficult. I do not expect to pass. Anyhow, it is in God's hands.

We keep praying for you.

Kind regards,

J(indecipherable signature)

Petit Seminaire PONT DE LA MAYE (Gde)

The cousin to Micheline: Exhortation to resist temptation—Pont-de-la-Maye, Thur., 24 June 1943:

Petit Séminaire 24th June 1943

+
Dear Cousin

The way my classmates have been anxious to pray for you, with so much zeal, has been very touching for me. They have been devoting themselves to your case for the past few days. I told them only what may be told and they prayed every evening with great fervour and piety. Today one of them was busy with it when we were saying the novena, so he promised to do it on his own, at recess.

Thus supported by the Lord who will hear us, I am sure, you will be strong and you will resist temptation if it comes. God is with us and He is fighting for us. Let us be united in Him against the devil! The Blessed Virgin is also on our side. She may be the one who will actually 'carry it off', for your friend may very well convert: let him not think that he would be disloyal ~~to~~ towards his parents: if he is looking for the light, he will find it in Catholicism, for it is the only truth and the only life. If it is ~~th~~ about Catholicism being a religion of superstition, tell him he errs, for if there are superstitious people under our denomination, they are in the wrong. You can see that all hope is not lost. If he is in search of the true light, he will find it with the priest who will enlighten him and put him on the right path.

Always united in Jesus and Mary

J(indecipherable signature)

* *

11

It was clear: the families of both parties were entrenched in their positions, and one of them would have to concede. Jacques had summed up the situation quite well with the allusion that conversion meant death. When he and Micheline met, they could feel the weight of silence through their reflective thoughts. Late one night, they stayed clinging to each other, speechless and motionless, watching explosions in the distance towards Bordeaux. German air defences capped off the attack with fireworks and searchlights over the river.

Finally, Micheline concluded it was she who would have to make a move. She decided to approach Bordeaux's minister-in-charge to see what his solution might be. This was a last-ditch effort, for Jacques' mother, the spouse of a minister, had been quite unconditional in her stance. The minister-in-charge would probably propose conversion, but there was also a chance he might find the situation 'sound and critical'. But then Micheline reversed her thoughts and imagined a total deadlock, an impossible status quo, and this put her back in the scenario where she would have to convert. Meanwhile, with this conflagration of systems, Jacques' case was identical to hers: from now on, regardless of what they did or did not do, they were traitors, traitors either toward their own families, to the other's, or to each other. It was in this context that Micheline decided to sacrifice herself and set out for Bordeaux.

*

The station was almost empty

On that early morning the Eyrans-Le Pontet station was almost empty. Beset by a sense of imminent danger, Micheline had become blind to her surroundings. Jacques was already out of her thoughts, far from her, and yet here he was, standing next to her, looking slightly ill-at-ease. He was staying behind.

With a heavy heart, a stomach in knots, and a head in a muddle, she was trying to decide what to say to the minister-in-charge, anticipating her annihilation as a Catholic. She had missed Sunday's mass and Eucharist, and now she was sliding down a one-way street. She saw herself at the bank of the Rubicon, unable to conceive of how the day would end. The fear of the void of her childhood had caught up with her: she was on the edge of the abyss. She was there, and it was impossible for her to imagine anything else. Her ordeal, her true agony, was only beginning.

The train stopped barely for a few minutes. As if someone else was uttering them, she muttered two or three words about meeting Jacques the next evening, back at the train station, while looking through him.

The journey constricted into a tunnel of emotions. Her whole being was dissolving into the endless beat of the wheels on the rails. As she struggled to brace herself, her palms were getting moist and sticky. She was nothing but a ball of nerves. Love, religion, everything had vanished. An inexorable sensation of ignominy had taken her over, consuming her like an obsession that her body was trying to expel.

*

Madame Hébert's sentences become shorter and shorter, interspersed with pauses. She is not looking at me anymore, and I am holding my breath. To counter annihilation and nothingness, to counter the destruction of her values, what could she possibly have expected to find at Rue du Hâ? I train my eyes on her, waiting for her to remind me that this is the street that leads precisely to Fort du Hâ ... to that prison where only a few months earlier, the guillotine had been in use, and where authorities had kept their supply of hostages to be shot in retaliation for assaults on the regime—I had walked past it twice a day during my first years at the lycée, after primary school. But now, even after I remind her of that, her gaze pierces through me. I have interrupted the flow of her memories, and I lower my head. She cannot make the link, being so absorbed by her dilemma, then and now, a dilemma from which there was no escape. The course she had embarked on led straight to a death sentence, with no possibility for appeal.

*

When Micheline stepped out of the railway station at La Bastide, a gust of wind from the river chilled her face; she was soaked with sweat but did not feel anything. The city of Bordeaux lay there, on the opposite side of the Garonne River. Peaceful, with its grey docks and warehouses, its black buildings, it was still standing. But all she could see was hell, the cold face of hell. Upstream on her left, the number of Germans protecting the bridge had been reinforced since the December attack on docked ships. She turned and, with a huge effort, walked to a 'gondola', a small, flat-bottom vessel that ferried pedestrians across the Garonne.

Between the two banks

Micheline took a seat in the boat and crumpled over. Struggling to control herself, she was finally struck in the middle of the river, between the two banks, as her bowels gave way.

She was shivering by the time she climbed onto the wharf. She now had to make a detour to clean herself off, at her college guardians' place, where she had planned to spend the night. Then, in a robot-like fashion, not wanting to waste more time, she resumed her journey to No. 32 Rue du Hâ.

When she arrived at the parish house it was slightly after noon. The building looked like a small cube, sitting at the crossing of two tiny and empty streets in the heart of Bordeaux. Micheline stood under an alcove, in front of a narrow door, and knocked. It squeaked open, and a weak, sickly voice, both hollow and hoarse, coming from the depths of some cavernous lungs, informed her that the minister was not in and, furthermore, that it could not be said when he would be back.

She had reached the heart of nothingness and a nothingness of the heart. This was a sign, it had to be.

She wandered from street to street, oblivious to the danger of roundups, and finally found herself again at her guardians. As the evening settled in, she was besieged by a new form of anguish, impregnated by the damp darkness of their little flat, even though her hosts did their utmost to comfort her.

By the next morning, a single thought had taken over Micheline's mind. Her body, drained of all energy, somehow found a way to take her straight to Saint-Pierre's Church, through a maze of putrid side streets, next to the port district, where the priest specialized in hard cases. Just as she joined the queue at the confessional, the priest was coming out of the sacristy, and noticed her. He looked her up and down, and motioned her to come right over.

Ten minutes later, she was sitting at a table in the sacristy, "beyond [her]self," writing to Jacques. She addressed him in the formal fashion and signed a break-up letter, with the priest standing by her side.

*

Madame Hébert raises her hands slightly above the table ... her mouth frozen, agape, as if in a seizure ...:

I felt I was tearing my heart out ... and his, too....

It is a short reaction, but it is there, squarely connected to her decision, made under a priest's counsel, and accepted fully as her own. She makes no reference to Jacques' absence or to the old couple's role in her turn-around. I weigh the strain she goes through to express this sentence, sixty-six years later.

Madame Hébert's first version of her memoirs only summarizes her relationship with the doctor, skipping the priest's guidance, and refers to this outcome as 'providential'. And now, again, she outmatches herself, confirming that written account as if she knew it by heart: "And before God I made my decision."

As I register this doublethink, I squeeze my tongue against my molars, waiting for more, but it is already lunchtime. I was too slow in reviewing the chronology of 1942 and 1943. We are now facing a chicken with plums and carrots. But before we eat, Madame Hébert summarizes again, in spite of herself, using the same words from her first memoirs: "Our notions of things spiritual were diametrically opposite from one another.... There was no way I could carry on teaching in the same township where the doctor was practicing...."

Outside, with lunch over, I come up for air.... Out on little, empty streets, I finally fill my lungs with fresh air, thankful to be walking in solitude.

*

The next day, I went swimming at a public pool, and then took the tram to have a look at No. 32 Rue du Hâ, and at Saint-Pierre's Church, inside, at the door to the sacristy. A few days later, I would be leafing through municipal archives to get a feeling for the war years. That is how I found, among others, a memorandum about a citizen claiming compensation from the city for his roof: it reported the allegation that the roof had been damaged by a parachutist when the Germans took over Bordeaux. I saw meticulous accounts produced by the civil defence with coloured-pencil lines showing the progression of fires. There were police reports on the citizenry increasingly refusing to use shelters at the sound of air-raid warnings. And finally, I read statistics on admissions to shows and cinemas: they declined suddenly by a third, and then, overall, by half, after the bombardments of May 17, 1943. In bookstores, I found information on the anti-Jewish exhibition, the roundups, and the shipping of workers to Germany. Later, on the Internet, I would find the positions of the sunken or half-submerged ships that Micheline could have observed when crossing the Garonne.

* *

12

It is not clear how Micheline got back to her parents, in Étauliers. When she reached their home, vegetation had fully matured and the garden offered some shelter from the sun, which was becoming quite strong that summer of 1943.

At first, while everybody was busy at some activity, Micheline could not manage to cover up her lethargy. She would remain in bed all morning, listening to the first noises coming up from other parts of the house, and trying to decipher them beyond their resonance. Two or three times she heard the voices of her parents or her sisters, arguing below, between the garden walls. She did force herself to participate in family life, but too often they found her washing her hands absent-mindedly, or staring into space, sitting idly in the shade of the vine and the calycanthus bush. It was obvious to her kin that she was not in her normal state, not because of her trial in Bordeaux, but rather because of the doctor's powers of seduction.

Home life, however, had to go on. Her mother, Madame Ponthier, not quite a woman of 'simple faith', had the strength of it, and she could be found on all fronts. If she was not ironing or mending, she could hold the fort at the store while her husband was busy at the workshop, or gone to the station, or to meet with a client in town. She had an apron for each function and she never rested for more than ten minutes.

The two spinster sisters, Aline and Cécile, had resigned themselves to the daily routine. They each had given up looking for possible mates at Remembrance Day, even before it had been banned. Cécile worked the garden for asparagus, lettuce, radishes, strawberries, beans, and potatoes; she also raised a few rabbits. In her free time, she would say her rosary or sing in church with children. Aline, the oldest sister, was in charge of cleanliness. When merchandise arrived in the store, she would disassemble the crates and the packing material for re-use; nails, ropes, strings, straw, papers, needles—nothing was thrown away. Aline was particularly attached to Micheline, and she had not become a nun to comply with a deal struck with the father so he would allow Micheline to do her first communion. She understood Micheline with all her heart, and could feel her pain. Dedicated to Christ to the end, Aline would stretch out her arms in the form of a cross, on her deathbed.

In the bosom of her family, Micheline began to relive her youth by leafing through old issues of magazines such as *La Semaine de Suzette* or *L'Illustration*. She could envision her dolls, Suzette, Fanchon, and Katie, and mentally stroke them with a finger as if to gain strength from their substance. Locked inside her was an ever-present feeling of oppression; she had never known this before, and it seemed unfathomable. At the beginning, she would often collect herself by a crucifix, kneeling on a prie-dieu and repenting as hard as she could. She was not to give up, for her salvation could only be in Christ, working at it through remorse for having considered switching to another faith. It was often thanks to techniques learnt at catechism that she brought herself into a state of humility: "Let us accept the presence of God and let us adore him!" And, little by little, she took in the relaxing effect of prayers, feeling a sort of abandonment, like a state of confidence and purification.

It was later reported that Aline, who could not stand it anymore, went to the doctor to give him a sharp scolding, landing the blame squarely on him. She found him in the middle of the street, and exclaimed, in the cryptic style of her time, "You knew it! It couldn't be possible!" Obviously, with such an outburst, a common stranger might assume she was alluding to the economic difficulty of two people living on a single income, or the possibility of the premature passing-away of the bread-earner leaving his partner without resources. But a second meaning was on everyone's mind.

Some friends took up Micheline's cause and tried to comfort her by pointing to new horizons. She learned from them that a Bordeaux municipal commission had decided to evacuate children after the bombardments of May 17, and that the School Inspectorate was looking for volunteer staff to supervise the convoys. Now that the Bordeaux submarine base was completed and operational, it had become a priority target, even in daylight. Though the base had remained unscathed, Quartier Saint-Louis, and especially Avenue Balguerie-Stuttenberg, had been hit, resulting in casualties: close to 200 were killed and 300 wounded, not including those at the Italian navy's headquarters, flattened by the second wave of bombers. Two weeks later, by the end of May, the first group of children, some four hundred, were evacuated southeast to Agen.

Toward the end of June, Micheline went to put herself at the service of the School Inspectorate. But as there were no openings at that time, all she could do was to leave her particulars.

Soon afterwards, through her connections, she did find a position as governess for the summer. She would be required to coach two boys, aged nine and eleven, living in a château upstream from Bordeaux, near La Réole. "Somebody" was watching over Micheline.

Each day started with mass at 6:30 a.m., and activities alternated between lessons and meals; Micheline ate with the owners. The children were perfectly well behaved, and Micheline liked to take them on bicycle rides along the Garonne. It was the season for cherries and peaches. The fruit were huge and firm, releasing an aroma that bewitched the senses. Their skin would let out a snap under pressure from the teeth, just before letting their juices spill onto one's tongue. As the three wanderers lay in the shade of the thick foliage hanging over the river, they could sense the quiet power of the current that had been ploughing and nurturing the land from time immemorial. One day, they waited for the tidal bore to come in from the sea, but it turned out to be rather insignificant for that time of year.

Micheline's heart and mind kept drifting through an inner landscape of devastation. Sometimes, she felt hopelessly drained by the effort of trying to avoid thinking about herself. And what about Jacques—what was he thinking about? What did he think of her? Had he started a new life? Did she have the right to know? She had reached the point of wondering whether her life would be ruined by her situation. Jacques' quoting of the old Arab haunted her even more. She had no way of knowing it also reflected the philosopher Averroës's position on things and context, without which nothing exists—being, non-being, and therefore death—and that the quote failed to include humanity as a whole, forming a context of its own. For Micheline, to come back to life through the subcontext she had delineated as hers, she had to pray: she had to hold on and not let go.

Barely ten days after she began her new position as governess, she received a telegram from the School Inspectorate telling her she was expected at the end of July, to lead a group of evacuee children to the 'fall-back centre' of Lourdes, at the foot of the Pyrenees Mountains. "From a Christian point of view," Micheline could not refuse. Her hosts were disappointed, but she put that aside in order to devote herself to others, crowds of others—and forget. Once more, "somebody was watching over" her.

Micheline decided to make a detour home before reporting to work, to get the right equipment for mountain weather, and in particular her electric radiator. She ran into Monsieur Iroz, who either did not suspect anything or was taking Jacques' side, in which case this would have confirmed that Jacques had received her letter: "Why did you leave?" he asked her. This simple question was disturbing inasmuch as it suggested there were possibilities other than those she had chosen.

It was around this time, that is, on July 15, that Micheline sent Jacques a second letter to explain herself. It is conceivable that she was troubled by not receiving a reaction from Jacques to her first letter, and so decided to dot her i's and cross her t's. It can also be imagined that she needed to dissociate her action against Jacques from the holy direction she was taking. This dissociation could be done only with arguments justifying her turn-around and giving her strength to overcome the person she had been, and survive. Withdrawing from her commitment to Jacques and writing the initial letter implied abomination towards another human being; she was trying to reconcile her action with her faith. Thus, to relate to the spiritual things from which she drew, she chose the term 'diametrically opposite', which called on mathematics, and therefore on science and logic. This points to a cognitive exercise aiming at a conclusion that was impossible to counter, one that had been initially conjured away, but now must be restored under psycho-social pressures. And if she had thought of being remorseful for having had the man who had opened himself to her truly hope, she reasoned with herself that conceit and vanity had led her to defy the established order and deride her religion. She was not requesting forgiveness, for Jacques did not allude to that later. It was only after these adjustments that Micheline was able to consider in earnest her contrition and her 'Grand Retour' to Roman Catholicism. Such is the contextual explanation at this stage for Micheline's second letter to Jacques.

The 'Grand Retour' proper was a wave of re-Catholicization that had developed that spring in Lourdes, to address the plummeting number of miracles since the twenties. It also matched the spirit of the new regime's reforms, for it was taking place with a "hope of reconciliation between nations"— and the wish to have hundreds of thousands of prisoners of war return home. This miracle was to be made possible with a newly instituted policy of shipping workers to Germany as a requirement for having prisoners come back home at a rate of three departing workers for each returning prisoner.

*   *

13

The contact who was to meet the evacuees at the Lourdes railway station was over an hour late. The air was stifling. Micheline's sixty boys and girls, aged between seven and fifteen, had run out of food almost as soon as they left Bordeaux, five hours earlier. Micheline and her two assistants were at their wits' ends to help the children pass the time. When the contact arrived, the air had cooled off and small gusts of wind rushed down from the slate roofs and the mountains. Unaffected by the haughty look of the 'gentlemen' posted outside a hotel opposite the station, the group proceeded two abreast through quiet little streets, to the foot of a fortified castle where the Hôtel de la Grotte stood. It was a clearing centre where boys and girls were separated, deloused, and regrouped by age. When the girls started to weep because they were about to be shaved like the boys, it was decided to use delousing combs on them instead, and it had to be done very gently. The children were then billeted in nearby hotels, up to five a room.

It so happened that Micheline's arrival coincided with the promotion of the warden from one of the health-and-boarding centres for boys. Hôtel Saint-André was a five-minute walk from Hôtel de la Grotte, on the other side of the river. His post was offered to Micheline almost immediately. As she was only twenty-six and had planned to return to Bordeaux within a few days, she declined. The staff, then, had her sit down, and they started over; they wanted to know everything that was waiting for her in Bordeaux. The School Inspectorate had no more assignments for her, either in Bordeaux or anywhere else, and it was too early to know if and when she would get a transfer out of Eyrans. The staff were opening her eyes. She also understood that by replacing the warden and enabling him to get promoted she would be contributing to the well-being of his wife and their eight children. Micheline was finally convinced and remained in the holy city.

And so, for the next thirteen months, Micheline devoted herself heart and soul to the administration of the Saint-André Centre. Within the space of a few months, Lourdes was to shelter and feed over two thousand children who had been evacuated from strategic ports and Paris. They were to be supervised by sixty male and female guides stemming from the school system, the scout movement and, to a lesser extent, from a pool of discharged military men. Their job consisted of insuring the safety and security of the children, stocking up provisions, and organizing spare time and education. As the children had become unusually docile in this new environment, their communal activities were made to resemble, as much as possible, those of their homes and emotional lives.

A group of supervisors met on Thursdays in the morning, in a maze of offices and corridors permeated with odours of nicotine and chicory. Discussions revolved around food tickets and grams in matters of Camembert—compared to plaster for its taste—, black bread, sugar cubes, and rare potatoes. Food allotments were always made in reference to whether the children were above or below age thirteen, especially in the case of milk. Beets, turnips, Jerusalem artichokes, and carrots were processed differently. In spite of this system of distribution based on equality of needs, the children were constantly starving, and so were the guides. One night a guide complained so much of stomach cramps that

Micheline mixed him some of her flour from Étauliers with water, and boiled it for him on her office burner.

The Saint-André health-and-boarding centre
Lourdes, 1943-44

Sometimes at the beginning, when leaving a meeting, Micheline would catch herself thinking about her personal situation and nothing else. This recurring burden felt heavier than her workload. During these first afternoons, however, when released from duty during the children's nap, she would go and gather her thoughts at the Grotto or at the Basilica, two hundred metres away from the hotel. She could also attend mass there early any morning, with the faithful who were somewhat more numerous that year. It was during the services, among the incurably ill, the disabled for life, or those with birth defects, all lined up on their beds and wheelchairs, letting out a rasping sigh from time to time, that Micheline managed to unload her burden, take time to reflect, and channel her vital force to the better-being of her neighbour. For really, the distress that plagued her lay also with others, and fighting that evil was fighting her own evil and killing two birds with one stone. Slowly then, far from any arrogance or pride, Micheline could start mending her self-esteem.

At night, alone in her room, on the other hand, after she had finished tucking in the children, when quiet returned to the city and seeped into the hotel, she felt a draft coming in through the window, and a sensation would re-emerge in her chest to the rhythm of her heartbeat, as to the rhythm of a life torn from hers, with a will of its own—the feeling of an endless, monumental, unfathomable loss—the curse of absolute emptiness, nothingness, and survival—the curse of loneliness and worthlessness.

Some nights, as she unburdened herself with prayers, she was convinced that this feeling could not go on tracking her for much longer, because her happiness with Jacques had been religiously incomplete, and therefore false. She started to accept her loneliness, for she thought she deserved it.

During the day, she would mingle with the guides at meetings or at mealtimes. Overall, the whole staff was uprooted, just like the children and herself. Most spent their days passing by one another, barely opening up, but still displaying good spirits. They were castaways allowing themselves now and again to jettison a slice or two of their former lives at dinnertime. At the beginning, as she watched them sitting around the table and waiting for the meal to be served, Micheline could picture them all together in the waiting hall of a railway station, in a kind of anteroom to the rest of their lives. This is also how another young guide, Miss Marche, saw the situation. By dint of orbiting around Micheline, she eventually became her confidante.

Gradually they realized that at least two evaders from forced labour in Germany were part of the staff; they were addressed simply by the names figuring on their identity papers. Another two illegals were waiting to be smuggled into Spain; once they had to be hidden in cupboards on the second floor when electricians came to repair a power failure. Like the French police, the Germans looked for outlaws, but they never found the dozen Jewish boys who had been given Christian names and were taken like the other boys, wearing their capes and berets, to the Basilica on Sundays to listen to choral songs. These songs were conducted by an abbot and young ecclesiastics, all natives from Alsace-Lorraine, in the Northeast, a zone that was out of bounds to returning French refugees, and now reserved for German settlers. The children would sing their own marching songs when going out on hikes to the Jer Peak or to swim in the Lake.

It was easy to understand that someone from the centre or the hotel had links with a ring for forged papers, or with a town hall delivering IDs. The cryptic language, the hints, and the unsaid were already well established before she took charge of the centre. The less Micheline knew, the better. On another front, a small number of those northeast seminarians, who had taken holy orders to evade serving in the German army, were turning out to be quite ribald, and an eye had to be kept on them. In the meantime, the Germans determined that crossings into Spain were on the rise and their police started checking papers more often.

Photo: anonymous, copy by J. L. F. Lambert; source: P. Abadie-Douce (via G. Piquet)

Micheline, her colleagues, and some evacuees
Lourdes, 1943

*   *

14

The 1943 dog days of summer came and went. Mountain hikes, tours, outdoor games, and religious services followed one after another at a good pace. Children wishing to take their first communion were given the chance to do so. One day, a young guide who refused to give up luxuries, brought back a kid goat from a mountain hike. This gave the cook a rare chance to prepare a heavenly dinner for the staff who imagined themselves sitting at a banquet. The children had been sent to bed earlier than usual, but they saw through the stratagem: Micheline had them return to bed by convincing them halfway up the stairs that a baby goat could not be cut up into a hundred pieces.

That was the evening when Micheline noticed a certain Claude, one of the forced-labour evaders, paying particular attention to her. For some time already, he had been in charge of a centre for enuretic children. From then on, they shared opinions and impressions that became their own little secrets.

*

As Madame Hébert and I continue our interviews, I am reminded of the children's story of Monsieur Seguin's goat that holds out longer than its cousin against the mountain wolf. Micheline, too, was struggling to hang on while in limbo in the mountain town of Lourdes. She would even survive, for now she had a second confidant, in Claude. But before I could be mistaken about it, Madame Hébert dots the i's and crosses the t's for me: Claude, whose real name was Jean, had a fiancée in the Périgord Province, and Micheline was not going to 'fool around' with him—besides, she simply did not feel any 'sexual urges' for him.

*

Harvests were not fully distributed by the time of the Great Pilgrimage to Lourdes that September, so Micheline and another guide decided to go and look for food in the countryside. They found farmers who gave them milk and eggs, which they gulped down on the spot. A couple of hours later, back at the Saint-André Centre, they were both struck down with stomach cramps, curled up in their beds.

The new school year arrived and with it the anticipation of teaching. Summer lingered through the windows of the hotel halls where classes were held. The teachers followed a more or less structured curriculum, and the children were taken on fewer hikes; and besides, some of them had grown weaker. In spite of the odd donations from the neighbourhood, the children were obsessed with food. A few started to steal or even run away, and the gendarmes had to bring them back. If, as on any organized school outing, the young evacuees picked up compromising leaflets dropped by night planes, the gendarmes would have to investigate and check the staff's identity cards.

October passed and November arrived, sweeping away the dead leaves. A handful of roasted chestnuts bought on the street felt like heat stored for winter.

At the beginning of November, like every morning, Claude and Micheline walked to the main offices at Hôtel de la Grotte to submit their reports from the preceding day and pick up the mail. Micheline found a letter addressed to her in a handwriting she knew. She opened it. And suddenly—"My dear Micheline…." Quick, who signed it? Jacques! "Your Jacques." He was there, in her hands!... The paper…. The letter…. Her hands were on fire!... The palms of her hands, her forearms…. It took her breath away.

She started running flat out … towards the river.

She started running

She was not going to …—would she? "Micheline!" Claude ran after her. He caught up with her in the middle of the bridge.

She burst into tears on his shoulder.

*

"But of course not!" That is what Madame Hébert answered when I mustered the nerve to ask if she had been going to.... No, no, she was not.... She simply had started running towards her hotel.... "Suicide is out of the question—suicide is outlawed for Catholics."

*

So, here was a letter from Jacques. For a moment it brought her pleasure, or at least relief. Jacques was not remonstrating with her. On the contrary: he was asking for forgiveness, or rather, he was getting in a muddle trying to ask for forgiveness. He had written the letter at night, probably late. He was retracing his steps just like Micheline, as if she had opened his eyes. He was echoing her position, thereby being united with her one last time. But he was also describing how he was looking for her everywhere after their "ruthless parting." He was not alluding to a return to the past, which was not impossible, but he was comparing the call of the heart, to which they had responded, to arrogance in the face of deified forces. All he wanted was one last word of forgiveness to keep in his heart, before obeying "humbly the Will of Christ." There was no reference to a possible conversion of his.

Jacques to Micheline: A request for forgiveness and first farewell—Saintes, Tues., 2 Nov. 1943:

Saintes 2ⁿ⁻ November 1943 (evening)

My dear Micheline

*I respect and understand the silence you asked from me,
which was as painful for me as it was for you, but here is a
missive disturbing it, and for which I must apologize,
although I had initially not planned to send it.*

This decision is not just due to the state of disarray I find myself in since our ruthless parting, and since your letter of July 15. As I write to you, I should not want you to feel, on account of my present situation, the least compassion or regret for what was done before God; I know how painful it was for you to write that letter, and then to mail it, and how many tears it cost you and is still costing you – The need to disclose this to you has been unrelenting since we parted; neither isolation, nor the wish to have a distant ending, nor sleepless nights and prayers, nor professional or family pursuits could dampen this wish, quite to the contrary, they made it grow into a duty that only a monster could postpone any longer –

This summer, on several occasions, I went to Le Pontet to deal with material matters of little interest to me, or for 'entertainment' such as duck hunting; these trips had no other purpose or hope but to cross your path - Last Sunday, while visiting my brother in Marennes, I went to the religious service as I usually do when I can, this service being concluded with Holy Communion, but I stayed stock-still at my pew in spite of a deep wish to take part. That is when I understood the cause of this turmoil, and so yesterday, I took the road thinking that for All Saints' you might come and visit your parents and possibly Iroz's. You did not come to Le Pontet, and this noon, I did not see you at the railcar in Etauliers. My thought was that God had decided otherwise, and I returned to Saintes on my motorcycle.

What I have been wishing for, for so long, is to be at peace with myself; in other words, I have been wishing for Forgiveness, but I cannot have this kind of Forgiveness, nor ask for it with conviction, as long as you have not forgiven me. I have so much to reproach myself with in regards to you, I have harmed you so much that I do not dare venture to ask for it from you–

If you think yourself capable of doing it, I should ask you to not send me a letter, but rather only a word, a tiny, single, little word that would be the last one, and I would keep it in my heart.

96

And then, you would never hear from me again. I am in wait for the conclusion of these matters, and then I plan a new start, not in order to put an end to a memory, ~ Justice from On High, but rather to do humbly the Will of Christ according to the knowledge and teachings He kindly consented to disclose to me for my stay on Earth –

My thoughts have always been with you, and so have my prayers, and I am asking again from the One who decided to break our pride, to keep us from harm and on the Straight Path, even if the thorns are meant to be sharp and many.

Goodbye, or more precisely, farewell. Please, allow me, one last time, to give you a tender hug

    * *

      *   *Your Jacques*

Micheline had explained her turn-around to Jacques, her decision to break her commitment, in her second letter of July 15, forbidding him to write back—and there he was, answering. The cognitive acrobatics she had engineered since July were in jeopardy.

By accepting to go to Lourdes, Micheline had chosen purgatory, and this was where she could not afford to fail. But she would know how to show herself up to par, and she would answer him. Because she had to answer. For a Christian is civil by definition. She would show him how strong she was in matters of resolve, and perhaps, beyond this, that she could be worthy of him. And he would answer.

Twice more they would write to each other, until Micheline's last letter of December 8, and Jacques' of December 17. Their words, in the end, did not mean anything, and they had never meant anything, except as contradictions of their actions. Words had enabled them to come into contact and to remain as such, on a transubstantiated path, the path of Christ, sublimating their respect for their own faiths. Neither of them would try to explain his or her contradictions and go to the bottom of the matter, except to classify them as wrong, as a mistake, as pride, even as evil.

In his second letter, dated November 11, which in fact replaces another one he burnt, a devastated, shipwrecked man comes to the fore, as vacillating as his handwriting. Still believing himself to be in a storm, he quotes the Bible and converses with God amidst his sleeplessness. He had suggested forgiveness from Micheline in his first letter, but now he is also asking for forgiveness from God, and if Micheline has already forgiven him, it is because she is endowed with the goodness of a martyr. He does not sign "Your Jacques" anymore.

Jacques to Micheline: The New Testament and second farewell—Saintes, Thur., 11 Nov. 1943:

Saintes 11ᵗʰ November 1943

My dear Micheline

Your letter was very beneficial to me. It comes—I know it—from the goodness of your heart, and as an inspiration to rouse me from my torpor - I wrote you a letter yesterday while I was still in the state of mind I had been in for so long—this letter shall be burnt with no regret. All I could see in your letter was your inner pleasure from having accepted a painful sacrifice that was asked, I am sure, by God himself to serve you as a trial. I am quite sure of it now. This trial, however, I could not accept, my mind refused to take it as necessary, and revolt was rumbling in me. I feel ashamed to admit all this to you, and yet it is true.

Last night, like yesterday afternoon, I asked God to come and help me, and enlighten me; I did not receive the answer I was conceited enough to think I would get immediately. But since I knew that in His Goodness He would give me an answer if I persevered ("persevere in prayer"), I humbly asked Him for forgiveness and I put myself at His service.

I awoke in the night and felt that God was asking me something. I left it in His hands and asked Him for the strength to understand His call. As I asked for His Light, I thought I had it within reach by my bedside. God asked me to read 'The Storm Calmed'. It was right on, I was in the midst of a storm, and what a storm to humans - I got up and took my New Testament; ignorant as I am, I did not know where to find the reference, but I was determined to find it. So I open the Book and right there, as God offers me a helping hand, I land straight on Luke, chapter 8, and my eyes happen upon verse 22, at the beginning of the account - just after a few verses on the Mother of Jesus - As I looked for more Light, I thought there might be another account, for instance in Matthew.

I first fell upon chapter 12, verse 46, and then, still searching, chapter 14, verses 22 to 33 - That was more than I had hoped for, so that I still thank the One who said, "Ask and you will receive" –

God asked me to write this letter, so I settled down and, in quite a fragile communion, I proceeded – Soon after, the light went out. As I am about to give up ~~and go back to sleep~~ *a voice lets itself be heard: "Be Awake and Pray" – A moment later the light was back - Words were slow in coming, and time and again this reproachful expression came to mind, "Man of little Faith." And the helping hand was there –*

To answer your request, here it is: You are asking me | - - - - - - - - - censored by Madame Hébert - - - - - - - | in the Scriptures, which is human and contrived – This I cannot, I have no right to this. As Luke says, chapter 8, verse 16, a lamp is not to be put under a jar (and even less so when this lamp is none other than the Gospel).

Up until now I was a barren fig tree, a beaten drum, not to say a weed. I admit it with humility.

In His bountiful Goodness and through His Grace, God would like all men to be saved; he asks from us, however, that we want it, and that we ask for it, and that at the same time we fully give the gift of ourselves to His service - To receive is much, and we have received a lot, but a lot will be asked from

*us and we shall be judged from our fruit and our deeds -
"Damned be the barren fig tree for it will be destroyed by
fire!" (even when adorned with foliage)*

*In my letter I was asking for forgiveness for all the wrong
I did you; your answer is to the image of your great kindness;
you forgive those who do you wrong the same way martyrs
forgave their executioners.*

*This letter, written with a pencil on some ugly paper, is
coming to an end; daylight is about to break –*

*Once more I offer thanks to God for having taken pity on
me, for having come to calm this storm, and also for having
kept you under His Protection and for granting you His
Peace. In the name of his Beloved Son who died for our sins,
I ask Him to keep you from all harm and to grant you His
Strength and His Light -*

*God's Will be done, and if such is His Will, all I can say to
you with still a heavy heart is: Goodbye—for this also means,
Till we meet again*

Jacques

In his third letter, dated November 21, Jacques has regained possession of himself, calling upon Micheline three times by her name (he wishes her a happy birthday). He makes two references to death (capitalized)—if he has been forgiven, he owes it to the mercy of God. Also, since he lost his practice, possibly after applying for the surgery in Saintes, he has had time to study theological works. After referring to differences between Catholicism and Protestantism as respectfully as possible, he alludes to the oneness of Christians—but points out just as quickly their different beliefs. He invites Micheline to examine her faith, to prove to her there are reasons for questioning Catholic beliefs. In the postscript, he sets the stage indirectly for a resumption of their relationship and reverts to his old way of signing.

Jacques to Micheline: Repentance, faith, and hope—Saintes, Sun., 21 Nov. 1943:

Saintes 21ˢᵗ November 1943

My dear Micheline

My last letter was only the account of a night, and since then I have felt that something was missing and that I had to add something.

First, that night was primarily a trial that I needed for my salvation; I had rejected the sacrifice that was asked from me and revolt was grumbling within.

I have been broken and the calm has returned.

Yesterday I was in Marennes discussing it with my sister-in-law. I contemplated spending a Sunday in Lourdes. All things considered, I preferred to abstain—you can understand why.

I always told you I believe in miracles, for God in His Goodness performs them daily. I believe that a miracle of great sensation is possible as evidence of God's Omnipotence when a person truly has Faith, and provided He so decides - However, miracles that happen in the depth of a heart, with no outside commotion, are just as great, and may later on be just as fruitful, if not more - What is the fact that a repenting sinner, who sees himself granted forgiveness by the Grace of God, starts following the Supreme Guide, unless it be a miracle?

I am saying this because in the last few days I have been reading in the Gospels about a whole series of miracles performed by Christ. One of them relates to the question you asked me, I ~~thought~~ often gave it some thought lately, and this is the miracle of Mass.

I do not know how to express myself and I do not want to harm you. I am asking God to have you understand my thought for your Good and your Peace within -

I know that Mass is the pinnacle of Catholic beliefs. The fact is that until the last few days I knew very little of its deep significance-

Two articles written by a theologian that I just read in a religious journal draw a parallel between Mass and the Lord's Supper. I do not think there is any bias in it and therefore I am including them as an attachment. Personally, I did not think we were so close, though apart – I read ~~a hundred~~ these articles very carefully, they will be more eloquent than I can be, and there is nothing I would add because they were a revelation to me -

Next to this are other differences that are just as important; here are a few that you are aware of: Can the Blessed Virgin and the Saints act as intermediaries on Earth between God and men, or is Christ the only one to whom God has given this power? The Gospels' answer to this question would be, in my opinion, the second alternative. With regard to other points such as Confession, forgiveness through a priest, penance, purgatory, | -censored - |, | - censored - |, | - censored by Madame Hébert -|, *you know what I think of them.*

I must somewhat apologize for all this; if I mentioned it, it was only so that you would understand my attitude of the other day.

If you feel at all disturbed by the above, I must ask you, as extraordinary as it may appear, to go and see a priest so you can submit your doubts to him.

We are human and we are weak; for us to stay on the Right Path, we must hold on to the hand the Guide is offering us, and at the same time not try to confuse our poor minds with considerations some more-or-less inspired theologians have developed through the ages into supposedly unchangeable dogmas, keeping us apart, and remaining mostly outside our comprehension.

I would ask from God, however, as well as from the author of that article, to prompt a few men from the various Christian sects to better understand this sentence, 'God is Love', as well as, 'Let them be one' –

It is both because of our human arrogance and because of the 'lukewarmness' of the Christian Faith in general, that this poor world is what it is, and that we are still so far away from the Reign of God on Earth –

A saying I have heard everywhere (even from the mouth of Arabs) is this: "To change religion is worse than Death." Also, to change beliefs is quite dangerous, for, except in exceptional cases where change is made before God and in accordance to His Will, without any mental reservation or ulterior motive, it is rather rare for someone to not worship again what was discarded. What then ensues is the worst of all, namely, the loss of all belief and all Faith—it is the Death of the Soul.

Micheline, I know I have been forgiven, I feel it and I give thanks to Christ, and through Him, to God his Father.

I have lost my position, I am now a supernumerary and have no practice; I am just as happy, for I have achieved another kind of Wealth, and if I had remained in Le Pontet, I do not know if I would be where I am at now—it is a true blessing, after the trial.

Micheline, my thoughts continue to be with you as in the past, and so are my prayers.

I am asking Christ to keep you with Him, along with your family and friends, and I also ask Him to steer your life here below towards complete happiness.

Micheline, may you receive my best wishes for your birthday, together with my fond and even, may I say, Christian thoughts.

Jacques

P.S : After all these letters, I am leaving it up to you to decide to put an end to our relationship. I shall respect your silence. If it should be so, I shall manage to get back on course with courage and confidence. Please be so kind as to let me know of your decision. I shall be waiting for it.

Your Jacques

It is clear from the fourth and last letter of this exchange, dated December 17, that Micheline had declined to continue the relationship. Thus, in Jacques' mind, they are both on the path of the will of Christ, the path of sacrificing for separation, offering themselves up in an ultimate orgasm of religious faith worthy of the martyrs of Christianity—because Jesus, in his great righteousness, wills suffering. And Micheline is not the one who really granted him forgiveness; it was Jesus. And Jacques is the one who, to sever all ties, forgives Micheline's oldest sister Aline for the vitriolic confrontation she had with him. But in spite of all this, Jacques still finds a way to draw a parallel with Micheline, to bring forth a common point on the human level through the person of Miss Marche (who took it upon herself to approach Jacques), and therefore to be united once more with Micheline—always Micheline. Here again, in addition to the address, where Micheline is not "My dear Micheline" anymore, he uses her name three more times and bids his final farewell.

Jacques to Micheline: Final farewell—Saintes, Fri., 17 Dec. 1943:

Saintes 17th December –

Dearest Micheline

*You can be sure that anything relating to you from close or afar cannot leave me indifferent—your life, your work, your thoughts, your worries, your material or moral cares -
Micheline, each letter from you is like receiving a part of you and gives me great joy - However, you must feel, as I do, how much they are hurting us, spinning out, as they do, an illusion, the illusion for us to be brought together –
In a way, we both did all we could, not all by ourselves, but each of us with our eyes turned to the Most High.
At the beginning, I thought you could come to me, and that gave me great joy; it was a time of great plans for a life in*

*common, but also the time when, all caught up in my joy,
I forgot momentarily the sacred principles of mutual respect,
as well as the most basic and sacred duties owed to God Our
Father.*

*Even worse then, when, after brutally offending Christ
who had always been so kind to us, we stood before Him,
supposedly repenting, but ready to start over - How deeply
He must have suffered –*

*And, as I was searching for Forgiveness, the whole of it
was being weighed in the scale, and the whole of it is what
Jesus pardoned me for last month.*

He wanted me to suffer, and I was left a broken man.

*Since then, in his bountiful Goodness, He has granted me
Forgiveness and brought me Peace again -*

*I know that you, too, have been pardoned and that Peace
has been brought to you again; our prayers have been heard
and I give thanks every day.*

*In the same way that you could not come to me, I cannot
come to you. This is not through bravado, nor through pride,
but rather through plain loyalty towards Christ.*

*He asked us to stand a trial, granted, but also to stand a
sacrifice, the sacrifice of separation. Let us not go against
His Will. He does not ask for trials beyond human strengths,
and if we are asked to stand trial it is because He is giving us
the strength to stand it. Why? Maybe he will tell us one day.*

*The day you wrote to me, on December 8, I had gone to
Bordeaux to meet Miss Marche. We talked about you and
about the On High for a whole, sunny afternoon. You would
not believe how happy I was to know that this young woman
is by your side. Once again, it is the Hand of God that put her
there.*

Love her as she loves you.

*Micheline, I do not want to abuse this poor, last letter,
which I would wish to be endless. I am asking Jesus, as I do
every day, to keep you by His side; my prayers go as well to
your young friend who loves you so much; to your parents; to
your sister, also, who harboured so much resentment against
me, but whom I have forgiven long since.*

May the light from On High shine in you and around you.
Let us be true witnesses, in joy and in trials, for the One
who came to suffer on Earth so that our sins could be
pardoned –
Blessed be the Christmas celebrations and the coming
year.
Adieu, Micheline; thank you for all you gave me, and
please, allow me one more time to hold you in my arms

Jacques

On the surface, Jacques' discourse displays his religious zeal and rationalizations. His premise is that to have a life in common, people must have the same beliefs. It is obvious, however, that in spite of his ability to analyze dogmas, Jacques remains unable to stand apart from them, and he applies their ideology to the letter. This allows him to intellectualize his relationship with Micheline and to quash both his natural urges and his belief in himself, the very belief that allowed him to envisage a life with Micheline in Saintes. The use of the passive voice, and the impersonal tone that is reinforced by references to abstract attributes, rather than to God himself, reflect Jacques and Micheline's surrender and their dissociation from their situation. Jacques falls back on the doctrinal dichotomy that refers to humans as being weak, ignorant, sinful, proud or conceited or arrogant, and of a 'poor mind', while God is described with the gifts of omnipotence, goodness, grace, enlightenment, and fatherhood. In addition to designating religious concepts such as those of God, the Virgin, Jesus, Christ, the Straight Path, and Justice, his vocabulary is packed with terms referring to the first Christians: executioner, trial, sharp thorns, suffering, martyr, and sacrifice (a reoccurrence from his mother's letter). The verb 'to love' is used only in the last letter, in relation to the 'love' between Micheline and Miss Marche; physical contact between Jacques and Micheline is pictured in the form of a parting hug, at the end of the first and the last letters, but to a different degree. When referring to daily matters, on the other hand, Jacques and Micheline appear to mirror each other and, paradoxically, by virtue of their irreconcilable beliefs, they find themselves irremediably united on the path of self-abnegation. Allusions to moments spent together are sparse; references made to the future are vague, except for the anticipation of the New Year, possibly indicating a kind of cult of remembrance.

*

Madame Hébert scans through these old letters as we sit at the kitchen table. She easily finds a few passages to which she draws my attention. She strikes out a few words deemed connected to boorish Catholicism and asks me not to reproduce them. With such reflexes still in action, I wonder whether she ever grasped the fondness of that man for her, whether she was ever able to ward off, even for just a short moment, the alienation of socio-religious structures and dogmas.

I just simply do not want the story to fizzle out; I want to know whether there is an aftermath. Of course, Micheline met Laurent, and she married him. She saw Claude two more times, Claude who had taken her on a picnic to Lourdes' Lake on a tandem bicycle they had rented after the shock of Jacques' first letter; but beyond these encounters, Madame Hébert spent over two of our four weeks together telling me about her time with Jacques.

She is holding Jacques' last letter with both hands, with all the fingers of her two old hands. With her back swollen at the shoulders, bent forward, she is now entirely engrossed in her reading. Silence takes over the kitchen. Her features set in concentration, she glides her eyes from one line to the next, without spectacles, over the stretched paper, a paper from another time, that a man touched, too, with his own hands, pouring over it all he could from his faith, his justifications, and his arguments, regardless of their abstruseness, a man who was already beaten at thirty-three, and claiming to be happy for it, making himself as small as possible.

I leave her to her privacy. I am not interested in the feelings she felt at the time. I am trying to gauge her present-day feelings, the effect of the past on the present. All I find are rationalizations. Is she discerning new meanings in these words, can she give them new interpretations? I wait for her verdict; but no, there is nothing ambiguous about her. She repeats the reasons for the irreconcilability of their positions.

And then, in spite of all these explanations justifying her entrenchment, Madame Hébert finally concludes in a barely perceptible whisper:

I wonder how I could.... I suffered horribly.

As I fail to fathom the discrepancy, she immerses herself even deeper in her solitary read. I stay mute. I simply note her reactions, but I intend to probe them later. At one point she starts humming something and asks me: "*Le Temps des cerises*.... Do you know *The Time of Cherries?*..."

Only later, while re-examining my copies of the letters, would I notice something at the bottom of one of them: three round and transparent spots, clustered and serrated ... dropped vertically on the page.

They never saw each other again.

* *

15

We remained seated at the table in long periods of silence for the rest of the afternoon. Madame Hébert held Jacques' letters before her, on the table between us. Was he still alive? She doubted it. I would enquire about him later on the Internet, but I did not get any answer.

I felt a certain emptiness spreading through me.

It was an effort to rouse myself. I pulled Madame Hébert as gently as possible from her reverie: "So ... if I am correct...."—Micheline had changed her mind in the space of forty days.

"Yes, it's a short time.... It was wartime...."

We were silent again. She turned to a photo album and opened it to a page with the black-and-white photo of a rustic buffet against a plain wall—the kind of photo one wonders why it was taken. Coming out of a porcelain cup, on top of the buffet, stood a tiny bunch of flowers: those first violets, as she had found them.

Silence was keeping me out of her world, giving me a feeling of lightness, while hovering over her scenes of separation from Jacques, as if they stretched to the infinite. She had provided all the particulars, she had nothing else to add, and still, I was lingering on, gauging the depth of her concentration, and the essence of its object. I was looking for an angle, one more question to ask, an overlooked detail, as if to pinpoint the ultimate 'why'. Granted, curfews did not apply to small villages, and Micheline and Jacques had been able to leave for Saintes on their motorcycle at four in the morning, but there was another problem: Jacques' carelessness when he alludes to duck hunting in his letter of November 2, 1943, when, as will be seen later, the police were checking the mail. What kind of weapon was he using if they had all been surrendered in 1940? Only the Germans had the right to hunt, and duck hunting with no other weapon than a stick and a bag was punishable by a one-month prison sentence (*Ouest-Éclair*, February 28, 1942, under the heading: Court of Summary Jurisdiction — Duck Hunting). This carelessness must have been more to do with Jacques' state of mind at the time of the letter than with his character, for in the case of the motorcycle needing repair, it is clear that he was capable of taking calculated risks, especially in times of shortages of spare parts (his mother's letter, June 7, 1943).

From Madame Hébert's reaction, I realized I was getting hung up on details to the detriment of the message. She was right; I was not there to get bogged down by a mystery hunt. And yet, their plan to settle in Saintes had been indeed a calculated risk, fully borne by Jacques, bearing not just on their union but also financially on himself....

And so, here we were, talking about Jacques sixty-six years later. He had not been the man of her life, but his memory was still there, and so was his spirit. This is why she had not been able to describe him to me, he had become a spirit.

It was probably the last time she would touch these letters.

"Today, with ecumenism ..." she tries to say. Yes, today things work differently. She raises her chin slightly sideways, pursing up her lips, and barely lifting her hands away from the top of the table.... Did she feel she had been ahead of the social regulations of her church? Had she sacrificed herself ("torn her heart out") for her religion, convinced she was doing it for her faith and for Christ?

"Yes, nowadays...." I leave her to her remarks, to her religion, I do not intervene ... and silence returns to the kitchen.

I have a photograph of Madame Hébert taken in her kitchen; she is smiling.

*

One stays loyal to great moments of hope. It seemed, however, that Madame Hébert would not have to bear the cross of her failed pursuit of love much longer. Told in only seventeen sentences in her first biography, it had been too painful to relate on the first try. But finally, after the shock of her grandson Yann's death, a new perspective had emerged.

Once back in Canada, I made a few phone calls to Madame Hébert to fine-tune a few points. But also, I could not let go the story of Jacques and Micheline. One day, after hours of picking over nuances, she showered me with a new set of explanations for her ambiguous position all those years ago: "Come on! The Eucharist! By apostatizing I was losing the Eucharist! Christ would not have been present at communion anymore!... It was death! Protestants do not have that ... and without that ... death scares me!" In other words, the explanation was now that Micheline had unmasked Mephistopheles at the last minute: she had abandoned Jacques in exchange for the Eucharist and eternal life. Was this the reason she had rejected the ultimate dialogue proposed by Jacques—and left him to a certain death, together with all the Protestants of the world? Had this consideration been supposed to supersede her concern for material survival should she have married Jacques? Wasn't this new rationalization, based on dogma and theological theories—irrefutable within its own subcontext—, keeping me away from another, more human consideration? The more I looked for some reasoning, the more I ran into complications.

At a certain point Madame Hébert let me understand that she had had enough of convoluted thoughts; all she wanted was to live day by day and sweep away the past.

When she met Laurent, nine years later, she would get back on her feet. It would be another story, somewhat like in a straight, conventional narrative, with never-ending pitfalls of the petty kind. But in the case of Jacques—the torments and torture, compounded with a sense of the irreparable, of an ever-lasting loss, of something simply vanished—all this, combined with the padded obstacle of the religious status quo, it all had come back to her.

Now that she had unburdened herself and her eczema and hives had almost disappeared, she dared to hope her story would make some sense under my pen. She finally began to feel relieved. By confiding in me, she had drained herself. There was no strength left to go back anymore. I realized that, in essence, this was, in a way, what I had come for, and it was up to me to testify to her predicament.

*

Eight years after their break-up, Micheline learned from a cousin that Jacques had married around 1946 and was practicing at Saint-Palais-sur-Mer, near Royan. Of course, she was happy to hear about him, and when she talks about it, strangely, her pitch gets higher and hovers with an air of nostalgia. Whether she feels it was a coincidence or a sign, she does not say. As it happened, Micheline had spent a week in Royan and Saint-Palais, soon after the last bombardments of April 1945, among the ruins, the rats, the makeshift graves, and the stray dogs that had reclaimed their rights over the German ban forbidding "dogs, Jews, and French people" to stroll on the beach. She had gone there to check on her father's cottage that was occupied by survivors and miraculously untouched.

And now there was a doubt whether they might have crossed paths, without knowing it.

After

***

PART III

16

The country was not fully liberated when the health-and-boarding centres were disbanded and the children were sent back to their families. The educational system was revamped and new administrative measures were taken to cleanse it of the previous regime. A warden like Micheline, coming from an ad hoc centre such as the one in Lourdes, was perfectly suited to be at the vanguard of a modern Republic, resurrected from the flames of war, on the verge of granting women the right to vote. This was how Micheline was called back from Lourdes to Bordeaux in the early autumn of 1944 and assigned to new duties.

Micheline took advantage of this move to reconnect with her family. She discovered her father had become bedridden and only had a few months to live. Her world was moving from one shambles to another. Now that the Occupier had been dislodged, the abominations of national, and sexual, treachery made religious treachery relative. During her visit, Micheline witnessed the spectacle of young laundresses with shaved heads, the symbol of damned love. This public punishment, even for one mayor's daughter, served as a warning to young Frenchwomen, the majority Catholic virgins. "Bah! If the men had been French, they would still have gone to bed with them ..." Madame Hébert said to me during our interviews. Only decades later would the heroism of one of those Franco-German love relationships be acknowledged for preventing the demolition of Bordeaux's port facilities at the time of the German pull-out.

And so, after managing a centre in Lourdes during the war, Micheline was offered—basically on a silver platter—two vocational centres one after the other, both on the outskirts of Bordeaux. Between these two postings, she did a short stint at the School Inspectorate, in downtown Bordeaux. Thus, from the autumn of 1944 to the summer of 1947, she headed the girls' training centres of Floirac, and then Pessac.

The Floirac centre was set up on a monastic estate, on the right bank of the Garonne. It was a relatively remote spot and difficult to service and heat in winter. The girls' dormitory had a stove, but Micheline's cell was in another building and had no heat. When the estate was repossessed by its owners, the White Fathers, upon their return from German camps in July 1945, the boarders and staff had to be relocated to local schools until a new centre could be acquired. That is when Micheline was reassigned to the School Inspectorate and made to fold envelopes, and to sit on a Purge committee. She took advantage of these predicaments to learn the ropes of the new system. This is how she came to work on the La Morlette file. She assisted the School Inspectorate in the acquisition of this new estate that lay on the right bank of the Garonne, up on the heights of Cenon. And thus, shortly after being put in charge of the Pessac training centre, she moved again and took possession of La Morlette for the Ministry of Education, and became its first principal.

It was in 1948 that Micheline was resettled with her boarders amidst a park, at the La Morlette estate. It comprised Morlette Hall and a mansion called Morlette Court, built in the *Directoire* style. They had no use for its farmhouse, henhouse, piggery, and the meadow with daisies for the cows. The premises of this new training centre were converted into kitchens, workshops, classrooms, dormitories, offices, living quarters, a dining hall, a record room, and an infirmary. In the process, fireplaces were replaced with central heating, telephone lines were installed, public transport was rerouted, and tools and machines used in the curriculum's trades were acquired.

Morlette Hall

From January 1948 to her retirement in June 1976, Micheline would be the lady of La Morlette. As the years went by, a few boys would be admitted to the centre and, with a recruiting area expanded to the surrounding regions, and the creation of half-boarding and non-resident statuses, the number of trainees would increase tenfold. The property size, on the other hand, would shrink to half, the farmer would be let go, and a new four-storey training building would eventually be constructed. A string of reorganizational measures were instituted over and over again.

The common-core curriculum at the Morlette Centre included humanities, science, art, and physical education. Syllabuses for the professional training of girls in fields such as cooking, hairdressing, and sewing did not exist yet on the national level, so these courses were adapted from Bordeaux's municipal curriculum. These syllabuses had been developed two years earlier by a city manager and the principal of the new boys' technical college, on Cours de la Marne, both of whom had been invited to the inauguration of the new Morlette Training Centre. It was in this context that the Education Minister's deputy had called Micheline a 'fortunate woman', during the banquet that had been prepared and served by the staff and trainees from the Morlette Centre.

Morlette Court

As Micheline was taken through all these reassignments, moves, and resettlements, her papers and memories always accompanied her.

But during the first full year of teaching at La Morlette—probably as a result of a long-standing detachment from society—a kind of a leaden fluid began to spread through Micheline's being, soon producing a feeling of being sucked down, under a weight of abandonment and emptiness. Once again, her thoughts dealt incessantly with herself and her life, to the point that it became utterly exhausting and hardly bearable. She wondered whether this happened to other people. By the time the school year was in full swing, she thought she was somehow different from the rest of the world.

That was the situation when Micheline had to be operated for appendicitis. Her psychological state failed to improve during her convalescence. A sense of drift and helplessness seemed to drag her into a world from where one does not come back. Once again, something was fundamentally wrong. Her doctor noticed her state, concluded she was depressed and prescribed an extension of her convalescence. She remembered meeting with the parents of a pupil who kindly extended an invitation to their villa on the Riviera. Three days later, she was by the seaside, under the sun, sitting in the shade of olive trees.

*

As the years went by, exhibitions and bazaars would showcase her trainees' skills. The first bazaar was organized on a weekend in June of 1950. It passed almost unnoticed, as the invited officials went instead to the funeral in Saint-Seurin-sur-l'Isle, near the Périgord border, for the wife of the principal of the Bordeaux boys' technical college.

When she added this kind of disappointment to her lack of social relations, she wondered whether her new position was really any different from that of a country schoolmistress. But it was precisely by remembering her past that she could draw the strength to carry on, to go the whole way and complete a task that had to be started over and over again, day in and day out, without ever missing anything.

In January of the following year, right in midterm, Micheline had her trainees' works displayed at the Bordeaux Fine Arts Gallery, along with those of the most famous workers of the land. In their midst, the stand of La Morlette looked both modest and daring. But Micheline's ever-growing duties and responsibilities were literally draining her. She stepped away from the exhibit to rest for a moment. As she was taking some fresh air by herself at the gallery's entrance, a man with a black overcoat approached her: "Excuse me, Miss, you are going to catch cold. You'd better go inside."

"Excuse me, Miss, you are going to catch cold."

She recognized the gentleman as the principal of the boys' technical college whom she had met at the inauguration of the Morlette Training Centre; they had worked together on adapting the boys' syllabuses into one for girls. This man had always given her the impression of being a capable administrator, with experience, and ready to support her.

They did meet again at other gatherings and events, and he would give her advice for the running of her centre. In doing so, they were laying the groundwork for Micheline's career, what was now the 'after' that had so struck her correspondent, the infantry lieutenant, eleven years earlier.

Meanwhile, in this post-war period sickness and death were never far away, placing another burden on Micheline. Her sister Marcelle had caught tuberculosis, and her husband was diabetic. She was distinctly reproachful when she learned Micheline was to leave on a tour of Denmark; no member of the family had ever gone so far. The fact was that a professor from the boys' technical college was organizing the trip for his trainees, and needed other adults to come along in order to defray the costs.

During her visit to Denmark, the sun would rise before five in the morning. The land was flatter than Micheline's part of France, and its people were relatively welcoming. She contacted a Danish student named Erik, who had been picking grapes the previous year at one of her cousins' vineyards. He offered to take her around Copenhagen, and then to meet his parents, who showed her how they could cook the French way. The two of them enjoyed a cruise aboard a riverboat, where Erik began to chat up Micheline. Later aboard a sailboat, he tried to kiss her while covering her from the wind. Undoubtedly her youthful looks, even at thirty-four, presented a problem, especially for a Catholic in a Protestant environment. It was so different from the Protestant area where Jacques lived. After attending a local mass in Copenhagen, Micheline met the priest and he summed up the Danish context for her in these terms: no, the Danes were "not a very practicing people." This was because they were a "happy people." As a Catholic priest, he could have said 'oblivious', but he said 'happy': the Danes were a happy people. And once again, Micheline chose the straight path.

*

When we begin discussing the 1951–52 school year, Madame Hébert appears relieved. I do not have to prompt her or ask her questions, and her voice gets lighter. This was the most significant period in her life.

On several occasions Micheline had begun to rely on pieces of advice from the boys' college principal, Monsieur Hébert, "the man who [would become her] husband." He would offer suggestions on how to solve the various management problems she faced. She was encouraged to "dig [her] heels in" to overcome the general resistance to change by her staff and the public alike. In one case, the hairdressing syllabus was redesigned for both male and female customers. Thanks to the trainees' parents, who were freely experimented on, a new professional licence was successfully developed, in spite of protests from the regional barbers' union.

Monsieur Hébert was a good listener, with piercing eyes. He was also a good conversationalist, and it was impossible to be bored when he was around. He had passed numerous competitions, delivered many a lecture before his peers, and published a book on technical training. He had not risen to his position by chance: he fully deserved his title of Officer of *Instruction publique* and, later, the Legion of Honour. He had a happy, childish side; but at times, he was an ageless wise man who had seen everything.

Their business meetings, luncheons, and evenings out grew more frequent. Little by little, personal matters were explored in the quiet setting of Bordeaux's Public Garden. They discovered they had points in common, such as an ancestry of touring journeymen, and a connection to the hardware trade through Micheline's father, and Monsieur Hébert's cousin living in Périgord. She saved the last hurdle for the end: "I am a practicing Roman Catholic, you know."

"Well, I am glad to hear that," Monsieur Hébert said, "I am a Catholic, too."

Their friendship was budding and Micheline did not feel like prey, as she had with other men. Granted, Monsieur Hébert was quite a bit older—he could almost have been her father—but his interest was genuine. He had lived alone for two years since his wife died in his flat at the technical college, he had just buried his stepfather, and his only child had her own family. It was time he took stock of himself, and he broke down, in front of Micheline, suddenly becoming Laurent, a weeping nine-year-old orphan again, not the gassed warrior persona from the battlefields of Champagne, but a man who was still mourning the passing away of his wife, the woman who had been his wartime penfriend. The *Croix de guerre* awardee had not lost his faith in God, but he was seriously questioning it. Together, with Micheline, he was now holding out against solitude amidst a social desert, frothing with religion.

* *

17

"Don't you find me too old?" Spring was over and the hot air of July 1952 had invaded every nook and cranny of the city. It was clear for both what the question implied.

"It doesn't matter …" Micheline said, as she leaned over Laurent and put her arms around his neck, whispering to him how happy she was. The message was decoded, the marriage was sealed. She went on, "But maybe … your daughter … might…."

"Yes, but I need a home. You'll see, she'll take you in once she knows you."

*

In her first biography, from this moment on, Laurent is "my future spouse" and "my future husband." Today, at this stage, in her retelling of the story, her relief is confirmed: a goal has been reached. When we were still with Jacques, I had detected a certain complicity between the protagonists, but here, now, I feel some apprehension that it is going to be different. I let Madame Hébert give me the facts that come to her mind, but at the same time I cannot help but wonder what led to this grand finale so quickly. Had it happened after they had gone to the pictures, when he had taken her hand? Had he taken it from under or from above? What kind of film had they seen? In which cinema? Was it during the day, or at night?

Gentleness is the word. Madame Hébert has rescinded twice in her life and I know what she thinks of emotional impulses. I should not want her to give me one of those helpless looks, as if taken aback, and ask me: "Why do you want to know?" In any case, regardless of what their professional and social relations were, Micheline and Laurent had grown closer together, beyond friendship, and this belonged to their intimacy.

*

Micheline told Laurent her story quite candidly. When she opened up to him about Jacques, she felt relieved, but also somehow, in view of Laurent's reaction, she felt she had acquired the right, or the freedom, to fulfil the need to remember, and entertain at leisure the thought that she once had been close to another man. From that moment on, without encountering any obstacle between them, she directed her affection towards Laurent. They both acknowledged their pasts were indelible.

"Oh yes, I told my grandchildren.... They know," she says as she points to the dining room.

But the memory of Jacques always lingered. She had kept his letters. She would feel the duality of a rush coming to and from her to such an extent that, at times, she felt taken away in the twirl of a higher power that blurred the individuality of the two men who would mark her life. During these moments, she would feel fully liberated but, at the same time, spread out, dissolved, and omnipresent through the immensity of this infinity that had given her so much anxiety in the past. The boundary between vertigo and rapture is thin indeed. The universes of Micheline's two love interests had aligned themselves and were now merging within her. Laurent tried to sum up this kind of feeling for her: "But of course, it's possible to love twice in life."

"Even God does not expect so much of us."

Laurent completed his story, too, for Micheline. Fortunately for him, he had not been summoned before a disciplinary committee at the time of the Purge, when the war ended. In fact, it was just the opposite. He had been arrested by the Gestapo when he was head of the trade school at Saint-Nazaire, in the vicinity of the German submarine base that had been attacked by British commandos, in March 1942. He managed to convince his interrogators that he did not recognize his own secretary's handwriting and was released, possibly thanks to his German-sounding name. This secretary had implied connections to the Resistance in letters to his girlfriend, and was deported to Germany. The School Inspectorate decided to transfer Monsieur Hébert out of the area "for his own good."

That autumn, he was put in charge of the Bordeaux trade school
that had been re-designated a 'technical college'; its former
campus on Cours de la Marne had been partially bombed and
taken over by the Germans for their railway *Kommandantur* in
1940, necessitating classes to be moved to another school on
Rue David-Johnston, near the Public Garden.

*

In spite of myself, this technical college from the fifties
appears in my mind, and I wriggle slightly on my small kitchen
chair, in Madame Hébert's home. My father used to take me on
the road from time to time during his tours of inspection. He
knew he would always be welcomed by Monsieur Hébert for
bringing him news from their Périgord village, even if he
dropped in unannounced, simply to say hello.

"Come on, let's go!" my father would say to get me out
of the car. I hated having to meet the gazes of the trainees who
looked much sharper than I. In spite of, or rather because of, a
two-year lead in my studies at the lycée, I was trailing except in
geography and, thanks to my mother's help, in German and in
translation into Latin. I was even more on my guard when I
thought of the first consonant of the word 'college' as
aggressive; also, I did not like the 'gravity' of the second
syllable, and the word 'technical' led me to imagine an
implacable subject.

Entering Monsieur Hébert's office was like entering a
huge, dark cave. The two men would walk towards each other,
as they exchanged a few words in patois. Then, once my father
had his friend notice how I, the "Half'n Half," had grown, I
made myself as small as possible to hear their conversation and
thwart any plot: I wanted to stay at my lycée. I would remember
overhearing, when I was little, Monsieur Hébert relate to my
father about jumping from crater to crater and from trench to

trench as a courier in WWI; I thought he looked like a fox, and that kept me on my guard even more.

"Now, in Issigeac...." When I heard these words, I would start to relax and look around, gauging the size of the files on the desk and probably comparing them to my father's. One day, in his investigative way of putting questions to rest, my father took me along and we followed Monsieur Hébert to one of the schoolyards where something serious had taken place. I do not remember the details, only my father's and Monsieur Hébert's behaviour and interest. This sense of location and history, imprinted in my memory, is what may have driven me in an undefined quest to visit Madame Hébert years later.

*

The weeks after Micheline and Laurent shared their past were full of relief and grand expectations. In the afternoon, around one o'clock, when stillness took over the park of La Morlette and the sun was high, reducing shadows to the minimum, Micheline felt more sensitive to the interplay of light on the leaves, and she understood that the natural way of life shimmering was a good thing.

Micheline and Laurent's economic future was secured inasmuch as they had reached the last echelons of their careers. Micheline contemplated putting Laurent in her flat at Morlette Court and eventually moving together to the three-room home for which she had already applied. They initiated the procedure for their marriage, to be held that September, and then broke the good news to their respective mothers.

They had previously planned their summer holidays, which they could not cancel, and went temporarily their separate ways, Laurent on his package tour of Austria, and Micheline, thanks to her brother's financial help, to the

Pyrenees Mountains, but not before she had organized the funeral of her sister Marcelle.

Micheline was finally able pull herself together in the mountain air of Bagnères-de-Bigorre, before taking the plunge into marriage. She had just arrived there when she received Laurent's first letter from Paris, and then all the others, displaying his fondness for her, as he related his journey through Austria. After his death, she would copy all of them out in her finest hand.

At the home where she was taking her holidays, Micheline formed a friendship with another guest, a young woman of eighteen or nineteen. She had been an orphan without a mother for ten years, but she told Micheline how lucky she had been that her father's second, younger wife had made a home for them. Deep inside, until then, Micheline had had a certain apprehension about her eighteen-year age difference with Laurent, but she now realized that she would have another, constructive role in Laurent's family. She expected that his daughter, Paulette, who was already married, would welcome her with open arms. This episode, which "took a load off" Micheline's mind, helped her feel more secure in her plans.

When Laurent came back from Austria, he was fresh as an edelweiss. Then, on August 11, 1952 he took a six-hour road trip to Monk Island in Brittany, to announce the good news to Paulette; she was vacationing there at her mother-in-law's seaside home. Laurent was also bringing a Tyrolian doll in his luggage for his granddaughter Loly.

* *

18

Laurent arrived in Brittany anticipating a warm welcome from his daughter, Paulette. Instead he was bombarded with arguments opposing the marriage. Paulette figured she had rights over her father, as his daughter, and as the guarantor of the honour of her mother, who had passed away barely two years earlier. This time, religion was not the reason: both parties were Catholic. Paulette was up in arms—assisted by her husband, Pierre, making it two against one—, firing off unambiguous arguments in a volley of angry shouts at Laurent.

On the matter of Laurent's deceased spouse, Paulette and Pierre launched their attack on two fronts: on Laurent himself and then on Micheline. The case of Laurent was simple: a man of his years was not supposed to remarry, let alone to a woman eighteen years his junior. As a stepmother, this woman would be barely eight years older than her stepdaughter. The whole family would be pointed at; the remarriage of Bordeaux's new mayor was still the talk of the town. The whole city would be percolating with gossip, and disgrace would befall the family. Who knew, even if the grandchildren were not included in the scandal, the position of the son-in-law, who had been a labour conscript in Germany, might be compromised at his shipping company. Weakness of character and mental unbalance were inferred. The daughter and son-in-law would have accepted an affair, but to realign the family ties was out of the question. It would have been so much simpler if Laurent had become enamoured with his son-in-law's mother, herself already a widow.

The case of Micheline was clear to them, crystal clear. She had charmed Laurent when he was at his weakest. Schemers, usurpers, fortune hunters—the world was full of them in those days, but the daughter and the son-in-law would not be conned by a social climber who was new in town.

Laurent was dumbfounded. The pain was deeper than it first appeared, and it would stay inside him and Micheline for a long time. Thirty years later, when Monsieur Hébert drafted the genealogical table for his biography, he stopped with his own generation.

*

Madame Hébert pulls out another box: August 13, August 14, no date—12:15, etc. She spreads out Laurent's letters. She reads in silence, sighs, raises her head.... She recites passages.... Her old fingers turn the sheets ... slowly.... Events were merging into a chain reaction. Was Laurent going to "abdicate"?

*

Laurent left Monk Island to recuperate on the mainland. He kept his head clear by staying in touch with nature, putting the situation into perspective. Micheline was distraught and wrote to him at the same time he was confirming his resolve to fight their blacklisting. Laurent had a new image of his daughter. He went back to the island. The *coup de grâce* was a veiled threat, packaged as a concession: "We won't cut you off from the children. And if you've made a mistake, you can always come back." Micheline would redouble her efforts to help Laurent rebuild his faith. "I am sure I am on the right path," she would tell herself, for this time she would not give up.

Laurent to Micheline: His daughter's shock—Île-aux-Moines, Wed., 13 Aug. 1952, 4 p.m. (barely legible):

L'Île-aux-Moines, 13.8.52 : 4 p.m.

Micheline dear,

[...] [W]hen she phoned Monday morning, I had told her I would have important matters to convey to her. [...] [T]he shock was real and tears were many [...]
Let me tell you my tenderness again, Darling—with much love,

<u>*Laurent*</u>

Laurent to Micheline: Their nonconformity and the upcoming struggle—Vannes, Thurs., 14 Aug. 1952, 3:15 p.m. (transcr. by Micheline):

Vannes, 14.8.52, 3:15 p.m.

Micheline, my fair friend,

[...] My letter from yesterday will reach you tomorrow morning with a rather short and colourless account of my discussion with Paulette and her husband. We resumed on the same topic this morning. My children's position and mine proceed from diverging conceptualizations and perspectives; it is impossible to find a common ground at the present time. [...] I am facing a wall. It is to be climbed over, or we will have to play for time so we can fully reshape their attitude. Of course, I understand the fierceness of my daughter's reaction in view of what she considers a betrayal and a sacrilege, when—in what she remembers—she has always seen me at her mother's side. I had reasons to see it coming, well-founded reasons, and this claim for exclusion, Micheline, can only be aggravated by our age difference.

*[...] I need your presence, be it just in thought. Our
liaison, or rather, our union, cannot be broken up. You do
feel that, don't you, dearest—and only the two of us can feel
that this harmony that so exceptionally took shape is indeed
"out of the ordinary" [...]*

*In any case, our spontaneous fondness for each other, so
deviant in appearance, will have to assert itself. [...] You may
find me bitter, Micheline, but no, quite the contrary, I am
fully convinced that one's destiny depends on one's
inclinations; to get off the beaten track of the social order,
there is probably no other way but to assert oneself as an
"abnormal character" [...]*

*Love me a lot, Micheline, and remember that my love for
you is serious and deep –*

Holding you in my arms on and on

<u>Laurent</u>

Micheline to Laurent: Despair—Bagnères (?), Sat., 16 Aug. 1952,
12:15 p.m. (last p. missing):

Saturday 12:15 p.m.

*Laurent, most fair friend, I just received your two missives,
and I wept—wept in disarray in the face of life and its
struggles. I had a foreboding of this trial. [?] I must bear all
this pain, so intense ... inside me. It is as if all the wounds
were suddenly opening up once again*

2 p.m.

*I am back, slightly appeased.
[...]*
*It is good that you told me everything, even if it hurt me a
lot. This will allow me to help you even more. For my love of
you, it is with humility that I accept my disappointment and
the immense pain to be considered a usurpress. If I had to
stand aside, if indeed I did, it would be so hard, but I would
do it for love, and this time I would be broken for ever ... [...]*

*I fully understand your daughter's reaction. [...] But
I would also like her to understand how much you need to
find happiness after having known pain and suffering. [...]
I felt that everything was waiting for you, that everything was
ready for you. There can be no break up at this stage. The
pain we both feel right now serves to tighten the unique bond
that unites us. It is not 'abnormal' to get off the beaten track.
[...]*

[Micheline]

Laurent to Micheline: His love and his resolve—Île-aux-Moines, Sat.,
16 Aug. 1952, 2:30 p.m. (transcr. by Micheline):

L'Isle-aux-Moines on this 16.8.52, 2:30 p.m.

Micheline, my dear friend,
   *In the foreground, foliage; beyond, the bay shimmering;
large, white clouds stretching; a light-blue mackerel sky,
a chill wind, and a quiet house where, in her childlike sleep,
lies Little Loly.*
   *So much for the setting. [...] [My last two letters] must
have made you realize that we have to get through this trial—
this new trial. [...] We shall face the facts squarely, dear
friend, and we will come up with a solution plain and clear.*
   *[...] I would say that we positioned ourselves 'out of the
ordinary' by assuming so spontaneously, in light of a
fondness—so intense and unforeseen—based on so many
shared responses, a line of conduct of our own. That must be
the image we project to all. Therefore, we are going to have
to build our life according to this 'out of the ordinary'. [...]*
   *And so, there must probably be only forces I would qualify
as 'short-lived'—including purely moral standards—
[working on] those who seek them as [on] those who run
afoul of social constraints of all kinds. Micheline dear, I am
quite weary and if I came to you, it is because I believed I had
found—in spite of your youth, and through the lessons of your
past—the true affection that a troubled woman in search of*

herself could bring to a fallen man, while in fact looking for
true, moral harmony herself.
   [...]
   I am with you, Micheline, I know you are distressed, but
you are mine, and I also know I am in love with you—and this
is undoubtedly an awful thing to be barred by others from a
second love—a so unlike one—and all this is so complicated,
my so fair friend. [...]
   Do pray a lot for us, so we can be enlightened.
      Keeping you on and on in my arms.
          <u>Laurent</u>

      Having clarified his position in relation with Micheline, Laurent returns to Bordeaux, lays out his plans, and launches the marriage procedure. He shows himself to be a man of action, optimistic, perhaps even a positivist, with a subtle skill for analyzing, and a definite one at strategizing. When back at his birthplace of Eymet, in Périgord, to pick up papers required for the marriage, he goes to visit his cousins, as well as his father-in-law, that is, the father of his defunct spouse, to let them know about his remarriage. Their approval fortifies his resolution.

Laurent to Micheline: His attitude validated, his target date, his daughter's concession, and his projections and paperwork— Bordeaux, Fri., 29 Aug. 1952 (typed in red):

                  Bordeaux, 29th August '52

Micheline dear,

   [...]
   Mr B***, an art teacher,54, just died in the space of eight days from an illness that made its first inroads a year ago. [...] Late last night I had to prepare the notes I read this morning at his grave. He was a wonderful man and now he is gone; he had been a widower for several years; he

would come to the college with a solemn face, as if already detached from the outside world. […]

But earlier, around eight, Paulette, my daughter, showed up without notice, not for conceding but rather to dig in. […]

Now that she realizes that my decision is made, she sees she can't counter it with the hope of a postponement to our union to test the strength of our attachment to each other. […] I gave her the [date] of late September. As you can imagine, this discussion did not go without copious tears on her part and heavy pain on mine.

Nevertheless, my analysis is that they would not oppose access to my grandchildren, nor to herself for that matter, but on the other hand, you remain out of contention to claim the same kind of acknowledgment. […] However, I think that this attitude […] will change down the line;time is on our side, and so are other factors that will come into play in due course. Overall, my daughter's visit of this morning, in my own home, seems to be an indication, albeit for the distant future, that she will not make an irrevocable condemnation and that she would not sever ties out of pride. […] And now, facing this abrupt loss within my staff, a self-effacing man who lay low for years, who gave up fighting and renounced everything, I am enticed more than ever to invest in this new life of mine, ~~xxxxx~~ the best of myself at your side. […]

[…]

Today, I sent for my certificate of residence at Bordeaux's city hall, which I will need for the civil ceremony. Next week, when I am in Eymet, as soon as I get hold of the other douments, I'll send a letter to Cenon's town hall. […]

[…]

I am in a rush, Micheline (I say your name so often so softly), I want to post this letter for the next collection.

Before I close, may I breathe to you once again, very close to you, very softly, the words that bind us, I love you.

And in my own hand: I love you.

Laurent - - -

Laurent to Micheline: Health requirements and the opposition's shift—Bordeaux (?), Sat., 30 Aug. 1952, 5:30 p.m.:

On this 30.8.52, 5:30 p.m.

My dear, sweet Micheline,

[...] I beg you to have a lot of rest and watch your diet.

I, too, visited the doctor earlier; 'a young man's heart and blood pressure', he said. I am also supposed to have my blood taken and my urinalysis done at a laboratory on Monday morning, and then stop by at the radiologist.

After that, i.e., once this procedure is completed and the results are sent to the doctor, he will issue me the certificate. [...]

After being at the doctor's I took my mother to my daughter's. Pierre was there. This time our talks resumed in a new climate. ...

Here are the main points –

- no conflict of interest at any cost

- my decision is acknowledged [...]

- [their] moral considerations and reservations concerning you are maintained but are clarified

- [...] I may go and visit them as before –

- in the event I am making a 'mistake' [I will be entertained again] with the same affection and have the same place as before

This was my answer –

- [...] pleasure to hear an adjustment was made [...].

- pointless to extend [...] a waiting period that would bring no change to my decision, a decision based on deep and authentic values shared in terms of morality, spirituality, and affective attachment, and that have been consolidated for the past 8 months [...]

- my strong invitation to them to watch us live together [...]

- [...]a desire for being [judged] earlier than later to avoid the brand of a 'legalized liaison' -

All in all—new, unexpected clarifications and a relief for you and me. [...] Together, Micheline Darling, soon, through our spiritual wealth and our love, we shall clear up this matter. [...]

Your great one.

Laurent

Laurent to Micheline: Paving the way for his employer's approval—Bordeaux, Sun., 31 Aug. 1952, 3:30 p.m.:

On this 31ˢᵗ of August 52, 3:30 p.m.

Micheline, my dear one,

I talked over two hours with M. [?] Bordas, the Sec. Gen. of the School Insp. [...]

Our two levels of administration are getting along well – We tackled many different issues.

And very discreetly I let Bordas understand—he is 57 and a good friend—that my life is going to take a new turn very soon.

He fully approved without me telling him anything specific, we just examined a number of situations and we considered them from a viewpoint both human and realistic –

When he and I meet again at the Insp. around Sept. 15, he will fully realize what our talk of today was about – [...]

This day is grey, slightly windy, Bx is deserted, and the green setting I am writing to you from is quite restful. That is where you are in my thoughts, making me realize that regardless of any conversation, even a sustained one [?] in all my activities you are the one who is constantly in my mind.

And do I ever feel these words from a romanticist—I am someone who likes them, these romantics.

"Sometimes, to miss someone
makes the world a desert."

[...] I love you, Micheline, with my whole being.

Your great one.

Laurent

The School Inspector was answerable for his staff's behaviour and, contrary to Laurent's expectations, he proved to be a major obstacle when they met again in mid-September. It is not clear how he got wind of the wedding project. Laurent and Micheline began to feel the weight of their own institution, as if they were pupils on probation themselves. They did not know whom to trust, nor which of their deeds would be reported. And soon, some of their close acquaintances echoed the position of Laurent's daughter, and their social network started to crumble. Tacit modesty in a certain society was the law.

*

The wedding was cancelled. The outlaws stepped back. The end of the year was coming, and so were Micheline's and Laurent's birthdays, standing like deadlines. Rain, cold, and darkness made October and November two quite gloomy months. Micheline and Laurent had no one to turn to, but when they met in the evenings, they kept a slight air of conspiracy in the corners of their eyes. "Contrary to popular expectations, [they] were holding on"—the daughter's veto had brought them closer together.

It was on a December evening, after dark, that Laurent and Micheline left their offices and met at the Cenon town hall. In a matter of minutes they were united with, as witnesses, a town clerk, and the bursar from La Morlette. After enjoying a dinner prepared by Micheline's older sister, Aline, Laurent returned home alone, as usual.

"'Thou shall not desire the works of the flesh, unless when wed'—hmm?" Madame Hébert asks me, wide-eyed and purse-lipped, with her chin slightly up.

The following day, at 8 a.m., they were wed in a chapel, with no other guests than the old night watchman, his wife, and Aline. Someone showed up briefly at the door during the ceremony. They never knew if it had been Pierre, Laurent's son-in-law.

An hour later, both Monsieur and Madame Hébert were at their respective desks, at work, and that night they were finally alone at Laurent's, together.

Twenty-four hours later they were on their honeymoon in Barèges, high in the snow-capped Pyrenees—on a three-day honeymoon. They had stopped pleading with society for their freedom—they had seized it. It was time to catch up.

Photos: copy by J. L. F. Lambert, courtesy of M. H***

Monsieur and Madame Hébert
Morlette Hall, 1954

* *

19

The following forty years were a whirlwind of events and activities in what is sometimes referred to as a full life.

First was the matter of a roof over their heads: the couple had enough room at Morlette Court where Madame Hébert had a four-room flat with her post, but the blueprint of the three-room home she had applied for as a single woman in a nearby neighbourhood, now proved too small for her and her husband. They negotiated immediately for a five-room bungalow instead, within walking distance of her office at La Morlette. Its construction was completed just in time for the Héberts to move out of La Morlette when the centre started to be renovated in 1955. They stayed in their new bungalow, with an extensive garden in the back, only for the two years of La Morlette's restoration and the construction of a new building. When they returned to La Morlette, they lent their home to a cousin of Laurent's who was resettling from Algeria, and later they rented it for a nominal fee to another family. Three years before Micheline's retirement the Héberts prepared to move back to the bungalow and started to have repairs made. They added an extra room and laid out the garden over most of the length of the backyard. Laurent was not a man to busy himself with flowers, so they ended up hiring a gardener.

The new training building

Managing the Morlette Training Centre required a lot of energy; the centre also had to be kept up to par by establishing new programmes, such as home economics and child welfare: "I managed La Morlette like a factory." During this period, Madame Hébert had to accept her husband's weekly visits to his two grandchildren and their parents. At the same time, her own mother was in poor health, becoming weaker and weaker. She finally died in 1954. But that year was also a year of reconciliation; after a two-year severance, Micheline was finally invited to visit her husband's daughter, and she accepted. "I was hard on you," Paulette said. Micheline took her in her arms. Paulette asked her to be the godmother of her third child, Gildas, who was expected the following year. Little Loly trumpeted the news: "We are all together, now!" Laurent had been right.

Micheline now had a family. She adopted her stepdaughter's children so well that she felt there was no point in having a child with Laurent. Year after year, Micheline would watch the little ones grow and learn how to pronounce her name; she would attend baptisms, confirmations, and communions, and betrothals and weddings. Together with Laurent she could enjoy the growing prosperity of the new France, especially after the franc had been devalued again. With the clearing of the river channels, the shipyards slowly resumed their activities. Every spring, a large-scale ceremony with an open-air mass, blessings, and band music was held for fishing boats sailing off for Newfoundland. American military convoys became rarer, and soon there were no more soldiers to throw chewing gum to little boys like me. Basements were not flooded in the spring on the heights of Cenon, but the snowfall of 1956 stalled everything, as it found its way into attics. Then the Suez crisis would reduce petrol to a trickle. At home, Micheline's brother, Rémy, retired to Étauliers to help his two spinster sisters, Aline and Cécile. And soon it would be Laurent's turn to lose his mother.

Nevertheless, life went on with advanced training courses, symposia, bazaars, awards to trainees at the Bordeaux Grand-Théâtre, trips at the end of the school year, sometimes to the Gouffre de Padirac, the Massif Central, and Paris. Micheline and Laurent would also make private pilgrimages and visits to Étauliers, and her parents' tomb. In the summer, they toured France by car. Laurent collected postcards along the way and filed them by region in envelopes; he liked to show them off to guests. It was still the epic age of the automobile when, from time to time, by the side of the road, especially in the mountains, travellers could be seen standing around a car, watching the engine spitting steam.

One summer, the Héberts pushed as far as Bavaria, and they found themselves invited as a matter of course to a peasant wedding. There they met two Bretons: a father and a son. Both had been prisoners of the Germans, but were now official guests, sitting across from a Bavarian, himself a former prisoner of the French. Both parties sat grinning at each other, unable to exchange a word. It is probably during such encounters that

Laurent became convinced that the French and the Germans had conducted enough fratricidal wars.

But for Micheline what may be the best memory of the post-war period is around cherry-picking time, when she and her husband were on the road to Royan, driving to their cottage at Saint-Palais, with Little Gildas, her godson, sitting on her knees, and their dog at her feet. It was Little Gildas, the one who later, much later, would pry open Pandora's box and, in essence, set in motion this biography by asking his godmother why she married so late in life.... But at cherry-picking time, she could feel everything was as it should be, and she would reminisce about travelling on board her father's light lorry on this very same road ... about her straw hat that had been blown away ... and disappeared into the dust....

Around this period, sometime before 1962, Laurent was promoted to Commander of *Palmes académiques* and Micheline was made Knight of the same order. One ate well by now, and one had fun. Wood-gas vehicles soon gave way to convertibles, skirts flew higher, and home appliances accomplished miracles, while Édith Piaf's raw lyrics vibrated in just about every street. No, for the tens of thousands of young men lost in Indochina, North Africa, and elsewhere, and for those of Abyssinia, Spain, and other places before them, all having survived their parents' world wars, there were no regrets. And the refrain would strike up again, more emphatically—as if to insist.

La Morlette could not escape from this gluttonous return to life and soon three trainees found themselves pregnant. Each girl was adroitly referred to Madame Hébert who acquired the reputation for being quite understanding, right from the first case. Trainees constantly discussed the pill, but obviously these girls had no luck getting access to it. Sitting behind a large, dark, and polished oak desk, with a small cactus pot pushed to the side, Madame Hébert would ask them if they wanted to keep the child, and if they wished to complete the curriculum. Except for one case where the parents rejected their daughter, ad hoc plans were developed in agreement with the parents, and in the end, all three trainees managed to graduate, have their babies, and find work. Later on, these former pupils sent photos or returned to the centre to show their children to Madame Hébert.

*

When Laurent retired, he started reading the Scriptures to the congregation at mass, and he offered his time volunteering. Meanwhile, Micheline, now forty-nine, would fail at an exam for the first time in her life—a driving-licence exam: "Madame! You think too much!" her instructor had cried out, "Let yourself go, merge with the flow!"

In the spring of 1972, groups of protesting students from Bordeaux, whose right to a military deferment had been repealed, came to ask for support from the La Morlette trainees. A strike ensued and lasted several days. The grounds were occupied and everyone sat on the lawns and listened to transistor radios. Madame Hébert remained loyal to her governing board, on which parents sat, and to the School Inspectorate: "They are going to take over the offices. The police are ready—they just need your call." Her reply was: "No. We just shut down and wait." Still, she could not avoid havoc when leaving La Morlette and students blocked her path. She came out of the car and had an altercation with a student leader. Unable to stomach his irony about the imbalance of powers, she climbed back into the car and had a fit of nerves, as Laurent drove slowly through the boos.

Earlier in 1967, she had been forced to put an end to the bazaars that helped finance the end-of-school-year trips. Now, the governing board went even further, opening the 'floodgates': trainees acquired new rights, they could smoke on the grounds and had Wednesday afternoons off—it was laissez-faire in all its 'horror'. That year, very few trainees graduated.

In the following year, Madame Hébert was promoted Officer of *Palmes académiques.*

Madame Hébert had witnessed quite a change in the world during her forty-year career. She, herself, had brought a lot of changes by turning her centre into a college with forty professors. When she delivered her retirement speech, it was with some kind of nostalgia, recalling all her years of labour, discipline, hopes, and pains.

Little by little, the echoes of her career—classrooms humming like beehives, feet stomping down the stairs at recess, the chanting of the strikers' slogans—slowly faded away. After a while, everything began to blur—Laurent's paralysis, the deaths of her brother and sisters, and the sales of her properties in Royan and Étauliers.

*

As years went by, friends and acquaintances started to take their ultimate leave, like voices drifting away. A void formed around them, slowly at first, then, as time advanced, more and more often, as if slabs of their lives were breaking off. It sometimes happened to Micheline and Laurent, either as a pair or separately, to regret having lost contact with some of these people, not having told them one thing or two, a plain, simple word, really, a word that, once said, stops time, seals a common experience or a personal feeling, summarizes and reinforces everything, but that, once missing, once too late, can be quite heavy to drag along in one's wake.

Lately, Madame Hébert has been lining up years in her mind. She figures that after Laurent's retirement in 1963 and hers in 1976, they had six years completely for themselves. Their lives had indeed unfolded in a good way. The sacrifice Micheline had offered to Christ in 1943 had not been lost in the infinite goodness of His mysteries. She had fully exercised her freedom as a Christian, just as she had heard it explained at one

of those symposia for Catholic teachers in the thirties. She had
done so both then and later, when she had accepted her spousal
destiny and given her husband unsparing care for a decade, like
a perfect White Beret hospitaller, until his passing away in
1992.

Micheline has looked at her life from all angles and she
remains satisfied with this analysis. However, she seems to have
trouble making it fully hers, physically hers, part of her body, as
if there were something against nature somewhere. At such
moments she can feel the presence of a man who once loved
her, alongside whom she walked and left footmarks in the
countryside, and who waited in vain for her on a station
platform.

*

She still sees Laurent half-dead and unable to speak, as
he lay on his couch for days on end. The telephone had just
rung. His daughter, Paulette, was calling to say hello. Micheline
was unprepared; she opened her mouth, about to give an
answer. Laurent grumbled something as he sat up, grabbed the
handset from her, and actually managed to speak: everything
was fine. And from that point on he started to recover from his
stroke. Madame Hébert gave me a full explanation later: "He
wanted to protect his daughter…. You have no choice but to lie
sometimes…. It is not good to always tell the truth—is it?"

*

The cemetery lies on a hillside, between an ancient bank
of the Isle River and a built-up area. Saint-Seurin-sur-l'Isle is a
quiet, unpretentious village. Family members and a group of
friends and colleagues stand around the grave. The coffin has
just been lowered and Monsieur Hébert now rests at the side of
"his wife" (sic), that is, Paulette's mother. The priest reads a
prayer and pauses. As the gravediggers wait for the signal, a

gust of wind sweeps up the hill, over the tombs. Paulette is overwhelmed with shivers and her husband puts his arms around her.

Micheline is not weeping; she stands erect, by herself, facing the grave. Then Yann leaves his mother's side and comes to hold his beloved grandmother by the arm.

*

Laurent had promised he would be with her forever. Madame Hébert does her best to maintain the home where his shadow keeps her company. But, still today, nothing compares to the void, to the immense void left by Laurent. The gardener still comes, and Micheline hangs on to life, as she says, because of Laurent's descendants who will be able to say one day, "I knew my great-great-grandmother."

*

I happen to have kept a photo of Monsieur and Madame Hébert standing by their front door, in Cenon, in 1984. The pair gazes straight into the lens, smiling slightly; Monsieur Hébert's stature belies in infirmity, and Madame Hébert clings to him, her head leaning somewhat towards his—for this man, strong, sturdy, the product of three generations of tanners, who loved going to work in a two-cylinder tin car, this man had fully understood her. The photo shows them as I saw them for the last time together.

As she related at the beginning of her first biography, right from the start of their relationship, they had shown each other their wounds: for Laurent, those of a wife lost, inch by inch, to cancer; and for Micheline, those of "the unbearable pain of a break-up, for spiritual reasons, of the desertion of a most dear and intimate friend." Laurent had exclaimed:

But even God does not expect so much of us!...

With Laurent's response swirling in her chest and head, Micheline had reviewed feverishly, in the silence of her privacy, in spite of herself, the whole film track of her sacrifice, her whole behaviour, her whole life.

"How could all this have happened?" she asked herself. Micheline probably gave in to fate and did her best to reconcile her conduct as a young woman with this new understanding which, if correct, was in essence sweeping away her agony, like relics of a wasted humanity. The fox had awakened the sleeping beauty.

Laurent's response to Micheline's sacrifice was the message Madame Hébert wanted me to pass on to other generations, I am sure of it. It also convinced her that Laurent's experience had led him to a higher power and that he was the man to follow. The fox had also conquered the belle.

Later, when Laurent was gone, after returning in tears from a walk through their garden, she wrote this poem for him:

Without You

Without you in this garden
Where summer's last roses bloom under a fading sun
My heart is filled with sombre thoughts
Nothing the same without you here

Slow was your walk along the flowers of this path
As you contemplated nature, meditated on the past
The world and death and life
Lost in your memories and long-lost dreams

Tired, but serene, you would sit
On the little bench by the crimson beech
Weary of an unsettled world
Far from the noise of the city

Without you in this garden
Where the last roses of summer bloom
I weep for the sight of you
In this haven of peace

About a year after Laurent died, Micheline and Paulette met at Saint-Seurin-sur-l'Isle. They had lunch at a country inn, took a walk together, and went to pray in a chapel. As they were about to leave, but still standing in the shadowy light, Paulette edged her way towards Micheline and let go a kind of sigh: "You made Daddy happy." They both fell in each other's arms. Micheline realized then that a chapter of her life had just closed and that, as she would summarize it later, she had "finally accomplished [her] mission."

On the little bench

* *

20

On our last night it was snowing and I jogged back to Madame Hébert's to return a book. It depicted the life of a young schoolmistress under the Occupation, and I had thought it might help me corroborate some points in Madame Hébert's story.

As I took my leave, I gave her one more hug, careful of her small, frail body.

"And so, you are leaving me all alone...."

In all of our conversations, this might have been the second or third time she was expressing a feeling referring to the present. Her large, dark eyes kept probing me. Whether this was a reproach, half a reproach, a disguised complaint, an accusation, I do not know. The fact is that it sounded like the conclusion to her life story, and the responsibility for it was falling on my shoulders. Quite daring, I thought, for she had let me understand earlier that, when I had returned to France as a teenager and lived in a boarding school, she and her husband could have inquired about me or taken me out from time to time, but they had not.

I returned her gaze and expressed nothing. She had told me everything she had wanted to tell me, and we each had carried out what we had said we would. But still, something appeared to be missing. For a while we seemed to be gauging what we were for each other.

Finally I said, "Yes, it is so—till next time," probably
leading her to believe that I was touched by her remark and
awkward at expressing my feelings. I slowly turned around,
crossed the front yard, and went through the gate to the street.
After a few seconds I heard her door close.

The tram started rolling down the hillside of Cenon. As
the lights of Bordeaux stretched before me one last time, I
sensed Morlette Hall overhanging to my left. It was there that
Madame Hébert had arranged for my last French meal forty-
eight years earlier, in the middle of the Cold War, right after a
failed coup attempt, and after a board of guardians debated in
council in Bordeaux for several hours to accept that my uncle,
living in a country "full of communists" actively opposed to
French Algeria, become my legal guardian. The dinner had been
served in a large hall, and at dessert Monsieur and
Madame Hébert, perhaps concerned for my 'Frenchness', had
offered me a French novel about the Canadian Great White
North, which I devoured during my first winter in Belgrade.

Now, while I was trying to make out the other bank of
the Garonne, where my last French home with my parents had
been, at the boundary of Quartier Saint-Louis, I caught my
reflection in the tram's window, gliding over the sky and the
roofs. I accepted it as mine, more out of a need for peace than in
defiance. Two days later, I would be airborne, next to my
woman—to Canada.

I came to wonder to what extent Madame Hébert had
influenced my life. Before I could find an answer, I felt her
story reaching deeply into me, far beyond her original intent to
educate future generations. It had metamorphosed beyond the
'I' of her childhood, as a mature and ultimate human scream:
"Yes, I existed…. Yes, I lived…. And I, too, suffered…." The
pain, or the obsession, of a forbidden love, the failure to come
together as in the story of Lara and Doctor Zhivago that also
ends in a tram—Madame Hébert had jettisoned it all through

the written word, and the process had turned onto me, the simple observer, because of my own experience.

Who has not experienced forbidden love in youth? Who has not missed one or two rendezvous with mad love? And how many have dared to choose the call of the heart, over social institutions or conventions? It was too late for Madame Hébert—she was a romantic heroine and somehow, through my solidarity with her, and in spite of my parents' path, I was finding myself in her. Just as Flaubert had been Madame Bovary, I was Madame Hébert.

Photo: B. L. Wilson

Madame Hébert
Cenon, February 2010

*   *
*

EPILOGUES

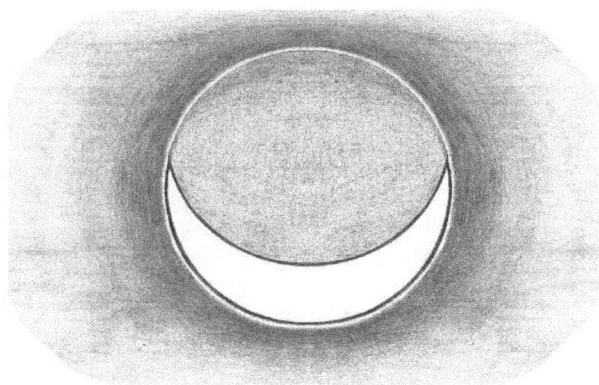

Epilogue

By fully confiding to a stranger, Madame Hébert had finally cleaned out her memory—'for the record'. The past was not hers anymore now that it existed in a written form, and it would be up to the reader, especially the younger generation, to draw a lesson from it.

In the months that followed our interviews, I sent her this biography piece by piece for revision, and three or four times she told me over the phone, "Hurry up…. I don't know if I'll be around much longer…."

Her confession to me did her better than the one she made at Saint-Pierre's Church in Bordeaux in 1943; her skin problems were nearly gone. At the beginning of the summer of 2011, after attending the wedding of one of her great-grandsons, she went to Dax, by the Pyrenees, for her annual mud-bath treatment. She was at peace with her body and her spirit. At the spa, thoroughly attentive staff helped her forget her loneliness. When back at home in Cenon, she felt a kind of serenity that allowed her to discover herself for herself and by herself, without interference.

Everything was in order. A life without a millstone around her neck was now possible.

*

Madame Hébert received my full manuscript towards the end of August 2011. She was pleasantly surprised by the title, in French *Paisible Garonne*, which means 'The Peaceful Garonne River', not far off from 'And Quiet Flows the Garonne'.

A few days later, I called Madame Hébert again.

"I am in shock," she said.

"... Oh, really?" I ventured, as some terrible doubts swept through my mind like brushfire; but at the same time I noted her voice was sweeter and weaker than usual.

"... Yes.... I'm.... I'm in shock."

I zipped through the entire work in my mind, trying to remember the difficult passages, to find where I could have committed a monumental gaffe, maybe two, maybe three: could my writing be salvaged? At the same time another part of my brain feverishly sought to come up with the next question, slightly along the active-listening technique: "You are in shock ... positively ... or negatively?..."

She let go a word ... followed by a few others ... and then I understood.

By reading *The Quiet Tides of Bordeaux* in one go, everything had come back to her. She was now the prey of an irreversible spell. She had been frozen stiff for the past two days. She felt she had been hit by an express train—it was a catastrophe.

In spite of a dozen or so errors, half of which she was ready to let go, her permission for publication was already in the mail. The real hitch that remained for her was this: now that she could picture herself writing the break-up letter to Jacques in the sacristy, she felt undermined by a new source of anxiety, a kind of feeling that had hovered over her all this time and that she had not been able to identify, but that now appeared in all its horror as the source of all her unanswered questions. I could not discern what her anxiety might be and, thinking that it had to be of a very private kind, I made no effort to prompt her to speak. Her voice was getting lower but, strangely, clearer in spite of the thousands of kilometres separating us.

Once more I was in a position to gauge the depth of her spirit when, in all her candour, she used the same word I had introduced at the beginning of the story, sensing her existential dilemma:

> I wonder.... I wonder whether the decision I made ... was really mine....

We finished our conversation, and as I hung up the phone, I felt the magnitude of her statement carrying me away like a tsunami. I realized I would not be able to help her anymore. I realized, with this late doubt of hers, that I should not have compared myself to her. It appeared to me that with this doubt, which was the proof of a reasoned humanness and of an authentic existence, the lesson she wanted to leave behind would lose its impact. Madame Hébert had put her finger on the epicentre of her life, namely, the contextual conditioning of the individual. She might have found grounds to exonerate herself based on the dictates of her faith, but by the same token she would be dissolving her individuality and reducing it to the nothingness she had sensed in her childhood. As a twentieth-century Frenchwoman, she had stopped fighting Christian guilt, but she still had to accept and take charge of her purely personal condition of weakness, as an individual, to break free of Nothingness and re-emerge as the woman she was meant to be.

*

I waited for the manuscript corrections and the permission to publish, but nothing arrived.

I called Madame Hébert again and we agreed that the mail was probably slow. When I finally received her letter I wanted to call again to reassure her, but strangely there was no answer for several days. At last, someone answered. A female voice informed me Madame Hébert was in hospital. She had been knocked over by an automatic door at the shopping centre—more precisely, by the two flaps of a door, one after the other, on the threshold of the supermarket, and had broken her hip. I was given her granddaughter Laure's phone number, and when I called her to find out Madame Hébert's whereabouts, I seized the opportunity to apologize about the scene at the door when Laure announced her brother Yann's death. Although I could not quite imagine her on the phone, except as a mouth speaking to me in the dark, I felt her goodness and a kindness in her voice.

*

These days I do my best to comfort Madame Hébert by phone from Canada as she prepares for her ninety-fifth birthday. She has now been transferred to a rehabilitation centre at Château Le Moine ('Monk Castle'), in a neighbourhood of houses painted immaculate white, a stone's throw from her home. Seen from the sky, the facility resembles an upside-down Latin cross, somewhat dislocated, lying at the edge of a park, at the end of a short driveway, halfway between the two ends of Bordeaux's Moon Harbour.

Madame Hébert's recovery is a success, probably thanks to her tonics. The staff members cheer her on: "You are a model to other patients—you do everything you are told!" Having been a witness to her own life, she summarizes herself over the phone, with a touch of irony: "Well, yes! I *am* a good pupil!" When I tell her that the Scrabble game I am sending her for her birthday is made of chocolate, she sounds a bit at a loss and says she will save the tile wrappers so she can keep playing with them.

Madame Hébert may still have the strength to meditate, in a small, sky-blue room, about the reasons for a decision made in her youth, but long gone is the time of cherries and reflecting on treason, free will, or the classification of Catholic spouses.

And so tonight, probably, in Cenon, in southwestern France, three or four kilometres from the Garonne River, around the time of the tidal bore, in an empty house on an empty street swept by an autumn wind, the manuscript of *The Quiet Tides of Bordeaux* lies abandoned in darkness, reflecting moon rays filtered by a window blind.

Yes … it is all there.

And he is there, too.

And he is there, too

Chelsea, Quebec, December 31, 2011.

Post-Epilogue

Nine months later, in June 2012, I went in person to present the final proof of *The Quiet Tides of Bordeaux* to Madame Hébert. This was almost a mistake.

"But I never said that!" Not only did she want to change many of the details, she also wanted to counterbalance the part about Jacques by adding events relating to Laurent. "I can't believe it! I must have had a breakdown!..." She challenged my two-paragraph summary: "Oh my, oh my, oh my!"

But, what about my notes? What were the facts?

After a thirty-hour defence of my work, sentence by sentence, I found myself giving in. Almost.

I needed some fresh air, far from Cenon. This time, I drove with my companion to the scene of the 'crime' and walked the platform of the railway station in Le Pontet as I, myself, had paced so many station platforms in my youth. Then we walked along the road to Eyrans looking for Jacques and Micheline's old flour mill among the vineyards, like my father might have done investigating insurance claims.

There it was. The sun had just broken through the clouds. Verdant rows of young grapes ran down to Le Pontet like shimmering waves in the wind. I stopped a few paces from the windmill, taking it in, like an old friend ... My companion went ahead ... Suddenly she turned around and made a sign:

right there ... among the wild grass ... at the foot of the mill's ruins ... were two small bushes ... of wild roses ... basking in the sun.

Photo: B. L. Wilson

Two small rosebushes

Back at home, by phone, Madame Hébert put me on Jacques' trail again. She wanted to know how to think of him, when she thought of him—as alive or deceased. I finally found the answer and phoned her: he had died on December 20, 1999. And he is buried at Saint-Palais-sur-Mer.

She had been prepared for this. But the slight delay that marked her reaction, the change in her tone of voice, and the low pitch that stifled the beginning and the end of her sentences told me there was something for which there were no words.

I looked pensively at the map. It was all there, everything had happened there, at the end of my fingertips.

Then I remembered ... Micheline wants to be buried in a small plot, next to her parents, in Étauliers ... in Étauliers, between Saint-Palais-sur-Mer and Saint-Seurin-sur-l'Isle.... I rushed to the computer.... Right—exactly fifty-five kilometres ... from each of them.

Lake MacDonald, Quebec, October 8, 2012.

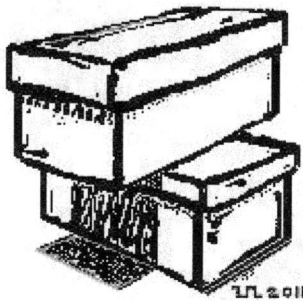

A Conclusion
written by "Madame Hébert"

I made a painful decision in my youth, induced by an internal power ... This allowed me:
- to fulfil myself professionally
- to encounter the person with whom I lived a happy union
- to live peacefully in my old age, surrounded with numerous, affectionate grand children

Paulette, Laurent's only daughter, who was tried by his remarriage to me, admitted to me some time after his death, "You made Daddy happy"

A distant past came back to my mind, an experience that made me mature, and allowed me to understand a man who had suffered separation, too, from a beloved spouse through death.
    No "I have no regrets"

This is the message I want to pass on to my grand children
    I give thanks to the Lord for guiding me on life's occasionally tortuous path

[Cenon, Gironde, June 21, 2012.]

Mais il est bien court le temps des cerises
Où l'on s'en va deux cueillir en rêvant
Des pendants d'oreille...
—*Le Temps des cerises*, Jean-Baptiste Clément, 1866

Short indeed is the time of cherries
The time to dream and go in pairs
And hang cherries from our ears....
—*The Time of Cherries*, Jean-Baptiste Clément, 1866

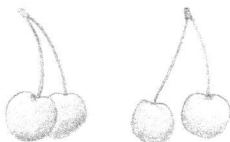

Socio-Historical Notes
(figures are approximate)

air-force cadet (in the context of *The Quiet Tides of Bordeaux*): A boarder of a paramilitary lycée, recognizable by a cape and beret. Two schools for orphans of 1940 aircrews were established, in 1941 for boys and in 1942 for girls. During the Battle of France, the French Air Force listed 646 KIAs and MIAs, and 364 WIAs. Over half of its remaining fighting force was withdrawn from the front by the new Pétain government a few days before the armistice, and redeployed to French North Africa; about two dozen pilots escaped and went on fighting with the Free French, under the British and Soviet air forces.

And Quiet Flows the Don (1934): From the 1928 Russian-language novel depicting political and romantic ambiguities in times of war and revolution. Its author, M. A. Sholokhov (1905-84), was a novelist of communist allegiance, and the 1965 Nobel Prize laureate in Literature.

apostasy: The public renouncement of a religion, usually in favour of another one.

Aquitaine: 1. An administrative region of southwestern France, stretching from Spain to the Gironde estuary, and from the Atlantic Ocean to the Massif Central. It includes five departments, two of them being Gironde and Dordogne. *See also* Gironde. 2. An ancient kingdom resulting from the break-up of the Roman Empire, bordered clockwise, from the south, by the Pyrenees Mountains, the Atlantic Ocean, and the Loire and Rhône Rivers; its capitals were in turn Saintes, Toulouse, and Bordeaux. After 877 C.E., it was reduced to two duchies, Guyenne and Gascony, which became part of the Anglo-Angevin Commonwealth (1154-1214); these duchies were annexed by France in 1453, and became full-fledged provinces, from the Renaissance to the Revolution of 1789, after which they were divided into departments. *See also* Bordeaux, Périgord, Saintes.

armistice of 1918: The agreement signed on 11 November 1918 at 5:15 a.m. to suspend hostilities on the Western Front at 11 a.m., and often taken to mean 'the end of WWI'. French military losses are estimated at 1,400,000 KIAs, 4,266,000 WIAs, 537,000 POWs, of which 17,000 died in captivity; in addition, 1,140,000 horses and

20,000 carrier pigeons were lost. Alsace-Lorraine was subsequently returned to France.

armistice of 1940: The agreement signed with Germany on 22 June 1940 at 6:50 p.m., and with Italy on 24 June 1940 at 7:35 p.m., to suspend Franco-German and Franco-Italian hostilities on 25 June at 0:35 a.m. It was signed less than three weeks before the German army ran out of supplies. French military losses in the fighting against Germany from 3 September 1939 to 9 May 1940 are estimated at 10,400 KIAs; in the fighting from 10 May to 22 June 1940, known as the Battle of France, military losses are estimated at 59,000 KIAs (incl. 12 generals and one rear admiral), 123,000 WIAs, of which 2,650 would succumb, 1,800,000 POWs, of which 1,100 were massacred, 70,000 escaped, and 39,000 died in captivity, and 320,000 artillery horses; civilian losses are estimated at 21,000 killed (half by the German Air Force, and 326 were massacred). French military losses in the fighting against Italy from 10 to 24 June 1940 are estimated at 140 KIAs or MIAs, 84 WIAs, 1,141 POWs. France was dismembered into eight zones (all ultimately occupied), the French city of Menton was annexed by Italy, and the Alsace-Lorraine zone was re-annexed by Germany. France was required to pay four billion francs every ten days to maintain 300,000 occupying German troops; she also had to hand over war materiel (except her Navy), release German and Italian POWs and nationals, and surrender Axis refugees; French POWs were to remain interned until the conclusion of peace, and a quarter of all French vehicles were also later seized. *See also* air-force cadet, exodus of 1940.

Averroës (1126-98): An Andalusian Moslem scholar and judge, also known as Ibn Rushd. He was a controversial philosopher and a commentator on Plato and Aristotle; in particular, he examined the link between context and being.

Balguerie-Stuttenberg, Pierre (1778-1825): A cotton-and-wine trader who, as a ship owner, was a failed slave trader, but met success and fame as a bridge builder in Bordeaux, Libourne, Bergerac, Agen, and surrounding areas. He was also known as a philanthropist.

Being and Nothingness (1956), from the French *L'Être et le néant* (1943): An essay on the role of free will. Its author, Jean-Paul Sartre (1905-80), was a professor, philosopher, and playwright of socialist convictions. A former 1940-41 POW, he became an underground writer during the Occupation and was active in the post-Liberation writers' purge. He declined both the Legion of Honour in 1945 and the 1964 Nobel Prize in Literature. Being, nothingness, and individuality are also explored in *Darkness at Noon* (1941), from the German *Sonnenfinsternis* (1939?), an anti-Stalinist novel by an ex-communist author, Arthur Koestler (1905-83).

Blessed Sacrament (in the context of *The Quiet Tides of Bordeaux*): The Eucharistic bread wafer (the 'host') that is displayed in a receptacle of precious metal (the 'ostensory') for adoration by the Roman-Catholic faithful, or locked in a small cupboard (the 'tabernacle').

boarding guardian: A volunteer who takes a boarding-school pupil out on weekends and liaises between the pupil's family and the school.

bombardments of 1940-45 in France: 1,500 areas were targeted by Anglo-American bombing strategists, killing 67,000 civilians. In Bordeaux, 34 bombardments killed 350, wounded 700, and rendered 3,000 homeless. Allied forces lost over 1,000 heavy bombers and 3,000 other aircraft.

Bordeaux (Bx), Gironde: Twinned with Quebec City in 1962. This inland port city was colonized by the Romans, sacked by the Vandals, the Visigoths, the Franks, the Saracens, and the Vikings (216-864). It was English from 1154 until 1453. Bordeaux has been the capital of Aquitaine since 1204; and of the Gironde Department since 1790. It was the capital of France in 1871, 1914, and 1940. A stage on the pilgrimage to St. James of Compostela, it became a Catholic bastion during the Wars of Religion; its Protestants were massacred in 1572. It was decimated by the plague in 1585, when 15,000 people died. In 1814, it was occupied by the forces of the Coalition against Napoleon. In WWII the Germans included it in their restricted coastal-defence perimeter. They occupied Bordeaux from 27 June 1940 until 27 August 1944, with some 30,000 men from various military and police services, including the highest concentration of SS troopers in France; 3,000 Italians were also stationed by the harbour (Sept. 1940-Sept. 1943). Bordeaux was the most strategic German-held port, the closest to vital war resources in Brazil and the Far East, and the furthest from British bases; neutral or Axis cargo ships and German and Japanese cargo submarines brought 114,000 tonnes of rubber, tin, and wolfram in addition to other rare products. To counter the Allied blockade and wage the Battle of the Atlantic, the Germans and Italians established a naval base with up to 75 submarines, an air base with over 100 aircraft, and signal stations protected by some 40 anti-aircraft cannons, balloons, and projectors, all linked by a network of 70 bunkers and pillboxes, and 70 boats dredging and patrolling the harbour and estuary. Nonetheless, docked blockade runners, including a tanker, were sabotaged by a British commando group using the tidal bore; its two survivors scuttled their kayak and withdrew incognito through Eyrans the night of 11/12 December 1942 (?); the six other commandos were caught and shot (Operation Frankton, one of the most daring raids of WWII). The submarine base was the target of over a dozen air raids. On 17 May 1943, one German plane was shot down and five Italian submarines were damaged by 39 USAF bombers, of which one B-17 was damaged and one shot down. Bordeaux's Axis submarines sank 104 Allied ships and suffered 53 losses and two scuttlings; seven German cargo submarines were also destroyed at sea. The German pre-pull-out demolition of 10 kilometres of Bordeaux's port facilities was sabotaged by a Protestant defector, and the pull-out was negotiated with the Resistance. The submarine base remained undamaged, but the harbour and channels were blocked for a year by mines and over 200 scuttled or sunk ships. *See also* Aquitaine[2], Gironde[2], Mauriac, tidal bore, Triangular Trade.

Cheverus, Jean Lefebvre de (1768-1836): The Roman-Catholic chaplain to the brother of the King of France. An émigré from the Revolution, he became Bishop of Boston, Mass., U.S.A. He returned to France after the Bourbon Restoration, and became Bishop of Bordeaux and Cardinal of France.

Conformist, The (1951), from the Italian *Il Conformista* (1951): A political novel on the confusion between normality and conformity. Its author, Alberto Moravia (real name Pincherle, 1907-90), was a novelist and journalist of communist allegiance.

Copenhagen Interpretation (1924-30): An observer's subjectivity according to which the result of an incomplete experiment may be postulated in an undefined or contradictory manner that suggests the existence of parallel universes. This view was countered in 1935 by the paradox of the dead-and-alive cat, making such a situation an absurdity. In the 1950s the debate on perception and reality focused on making distinctions between different possibilities and keeping them apart from each other in order to provide consistent narratives.

Doctor Zhivago (1958): From the 1957 Russian-language novel on individualism and the search for companionship. Its author, Boris Pasternak (1880-1960), was a poet and novelist who declined the 1958 Nobel Prize in Literature.

ecumenism: A movement toward Christian unity, with a modern phase initiated by Protestants around 1929, and borrowed by Roman Catholics during Vatican II, in 1962-65.

educational reforms (in the context of *The Quiet Tides of Bordeaux*): 1. 1924-36: Equality of access for boys and girls; compulsory primary education extended to age 14; grants for primary pupils; entry exam for secondary education; free secondary education. 2. 1940-44: Introduction of religious education explored; transfer of upper primary education to secondary education; secondary education fees; discriminatory access to education and grants; abolition of teachers' colleges.

Es war ein Edelweiss (1939), known in English as *It was an Edelweiss*: A German-army marching song. Its author, Herms Niel (real name Nielebock, 1888-1954), was a composer of national-socialist allegiance.

Étauliers, Gironde (Bec-d'Ambès, 1793-95): A stage on the pilgrimage to St. James of Compostela. It is the site of a French defeat in 1814 by the Anglo-Portuguese and Brunswick Coalition forces of Lord Dalhousie; it was occupied by the Germans from 27 June 1940 until 31 July 1944. Étauliers is located halfway between Saint-Palais-sur-Mer (where Jacques is buried) and Saint-Seurin-sur-l'Isle (where Laurent is buried).

Eucharist: 1. The rite from the 1st century, usually associated with Catholic worship (the 'mass'), based on the dogma of transubstantiation (ca. 1130 and 1551), namely, the substitution of physicochemical elements, during which an officiant offers a bread wafer to the faithful to be consumed as the body of Christ (the re-sacrificing of Jesus of Nazareth). For most Orthodox, it corresponds to the 'Eucharistic Liturgy' and is part of the 'Divine Liturgy' based on the 1672 dogma of transubstantiation (or transelementation, or reordination, or mysteries). For most Protestants, it corresponds to 'Holy Communion' and is part of the '(worship) service' (or 'Divine Service') and based on the dogma of consubstantiation (ca. 1300 and 1520), namely, the production of a spiritual presence, or on commemorative symbolism (or, since ca.

1965, on that of transignification). 2. The bread and wine used in the Eucharist.

exodus of 1940 (10 May – 20 June 1940): The flight of eight million civilians from their homes in Holland, Belgium, Luxembourg, and France along French roads, blocking the French army. Many of these refugees were strafed and killed by the German Air Force (10,000), thousands of animals were abandoned, and 90,000 children were reported lost. *See also* armistice of 1940.

Eymet, Dordogne: An ancient Roman settlement and a stage on the pilgrimage to St. James of Compostela. It was annexed by France in 1271, after the extermination of Albigensian heretics. Eymet was English by treaty from 1279 until 1451, but was disputed by the French in the period 1337-80. It was a Protestant town from 1535 until 1685; the Protestant church was demolished in 1671 (before the Edict of Fontainebleau of 1685) and rebuilt in 1808. The cemetery wall separating the Roman-Catholic tombs from the Protestant tombs was knocked down after WWI.

fall-back centre (in the context of *The Quiet Tides of Bordeaux*): An inland urban area equipped with requisitioned facilities, turned into health-and-boarding centres or camps, to accommodate school-age children evacuated from Anglo-American bombing targets. By the end of November 1943, 150,000 French children were reported officially relocated to these centres. *See also* Lourdes.

Flaubert, Gustave (1821-80): A French naturalist novelist, the author of *Madame Bovary*, a novel published in 1857 on romantic attitudes within the middle class.

Forced Labour Service—*see* Service du travail obligatoire.

Foucauld, Charles de (1858-1916): A French soldier who returned to Catholicism and became an antislavery missionary in the Sahara, and a lexicographer (Tuareg-French). He was killed while taken hostage by pro-Turkish tribesmen, refusing to renounce his faith.

Gestapo (*Geheime Staatspolizei*), or 'State Secret Police' (1933-45): The German political police, and its French branch (1941-44).

Gironde: 1. The largest estuary in western Europe, formed by the confluence of the Garonne and Dordogne Rivers. *See also* tidal bore. 2. The largest French territorial department, with Bordeaux as its capital; it was created and named in 1790, then renamed Bec-d'Ambès from 1793 until 1795. *See also* Aquitaine[1], Bordeaux. 3. The middle-class political group that favoured decentralization and, initially, the Revolution (1791-93); most of its members, the Girondists, were guillotined or committed suicide.

hennin: A tall, cone-shaped headdress with a veil hanging from its top; a supposed derivation of Oriental headdresses, it was worn by aristocratic women in Western Europe in the 15th century.

Holy Communion: A rite associated with Protestant worship. *See also* Eucharist.

Hundred Years' Wars (1159-1299, 1337-1453, 1689-1815): Three intermittent wars waged between England and France, and between their allies, over succession, and territorial and colonial interests.

Johnston, David (1789-1858): A Bordelais native and the adopted son of a prosperous Irish Protestant merchant of Scottish descent. He was a manufacturer of china and instituted a retirement fund and health insurance for his 700 employees, as well as free education for their children. He was a patron of the arts and he eventually became mayor of Bordeaux (1838-42).

Jonzac, Charente-Maritime (Charente-Inférieure [1790-1941]): A city occupied by the Germans on 23 June 1940. The underground ammunition depot of the German navy for the Atlantic was set on fire by two French workers in June-July 1944. The liberation of Jonzac, from 13 August to 1st September 1944, was hampered by German commandos from Royan.

Kommandantur (in the context of *The Quiet Tides of Bordeaux*): A German army command post controlling the occupation and defence of a conquered area.

La Porte étroite ('The Narrow Door', 1909), known in English as *Strait is the Gate*: A novel by André Gide (1869-1951) satirizing self-sacrifice aimed at achieving holiness (according to Henri Ghéon, the author's companion).

La Rochelle, Charente-Maritime (Charente-Inférieure [1790-1941]): An ancient Templar port bitterly disputed during the first Hundred Years' War (1159-1299), and the last Protestant bastion to be subjugated by Roman Catholics in 1628. It was occupied by the Germans from 23 June 1940 until 7 May 1945, and held one of the first courts martial to condemn to death a French saboteur; the pre-surrender demolition of its port facilities was sabotaged by a German sailor, and the submarine base was surrendered peacefully to French troops on 7-8 May 1945. *See also* Triangular Trade.

Le Radeau de la Méduse (1819), known in English as *The Raft of the Medusa* : A painting by Théodore Géricault (1791-1824) depicting the last survivors of the shipwrecked frigate La Méduse, part of a flotilla sent to re-establish French trading posts in Senegal in 1816. (Medusa is a Greek mythological figure who was cursed by Athena; all those who gazed into her eyes were turned into stone.)

Le Temps des cerises (1866), known in English as *The Time of Cherries*: A song on the theme of lost love. Its author, Jean-Baptiste Clément (1836-1903), dedicated it to a Paris-Commune nurse killed by the new Republicans in 1871. It was sung by Charles Trenet in 1942 and by Yves Montand in 1955.

Lourdes, Hautes-Pyrénées: A city by the Spanish border. After 1858, it became the most important destination for Roman-Catholic pilgrimages in France. It was occupied by the Germans from mid-November 1942 until 19 August 1944. At the time, it had the third highest number of hotels in France; 31 hotels were used as health-and-boarding centres for 2,000 evacuee children, of which 121 came from Bordeaux. (Young Jews in the centres were given different identities. Out of the 20,000 continental Europeans who protected Jews in WWII, 3,542 were French, of which 225 were in Aquitaine.) *See also* fall-back centre.

Maréchal, nous voilà ! (1941), by André Montagard (1887-1963), known in English as *Marshal, Here We Are!*: The unofficial hymn of the French State (1940-44), instituted for the glory of its head, Marshal Pétain (1856-1951), after the overthrow of the republican regime. It was frequently broadcast over the radio and sung in youth camps and schools.

Mauriac, François (1885-1970): A novelist of Roman-Catholic affiliation, born in Bordeaux. He wrote for the underground during the Occupation and was active in the writers' purge after the Liberation. He was the 1952 Nobel Prize laureate in Literature, and awarded the Legion of Honour in 1958.

Monsieur Seguin's Goat (1898), from the French *La Chèvre de Monsieur Seguin* (1866): An allegory by Alphonse Daudet meant to support conservatism and restricted freedom.

Moon Harbour: The name given to Bordeaux's harbour after it was relocated in the 14th century from the lake made by the Devèze River, to outside the city walls at the point where the Devèze entered the Garonne River. The harbour was set up on a bend of the Garonne caused by the Cenon escarpment, its shape reminiscent of a moon crescent. The lake on the Devèze was later filled in and Saint-Pierre's Church was built over it, in honour of Peter the

Fisherman. The crescent is reproduced on the city's coat of arms.

narrow door—*see La Porte étroite.*

National Relief—*see* Secours national.

No, I Have No Regrets—*see Non, je ne regrette rien.*

Non, je ne regrette rien (1956), by Michel Vaucaire (1904-80), known in English as *No, I Have No Regrets*: An existential song of self-assertion and of liberation from good and bad decisions and memories through the regenerating fire of love. It was dedicated to the Foreign Legion by Édith Piaf in 1960.

Pandora's box: In Greek mythology, a container filled with all the evils of the world and offered as a gift to the first woman, Pandora ('All-Giving'), by Zeus, the king of the gods. First mentioned in Hesiod's *Works and Days* (ca. 700 BCE).

Pascal, Blaise (1623-62): A mathematician, physicist, and philosopher of Roman-Catholic affiliation. He was the author of *Pensées* (1670), a posthumous apology of the Christian religion.

Périgord: An ancient county, part of Guyenne (middle, then north, Aquitaine), with Périgueux as its capital. It was renamed Dordogne, the third largest department in France, in 1790. *See also* Aquitaine.

Piaf, Édith (1915-63): A popular Parisian singer, best known for *Non, je ne regrette rien.*

prie-dieu: A short wooden stand equipped on the front with a low surface for kneeling upon and praying; in France, it often resembles a chair.

purgatory: A concept developed by Catholics in the 13th century to designate a place between Heaven and Hell where souls undergo purification after death. This concept was rejected by the Orthodox and Protestant Churches.

Purge Commissions (1943-46 [?]): Commissions instituted by the government of the Resistance, modelled on the Pétainist system. Their purpose was to exclude from power persons suspected of Pétainism or of collaborating with the occupying powers. They processed over 311,000 cases, of which 5,091 dealt with education. Suspects were referred to the new judiciary in accordance with retroactive ordinances. Nearly 800 capital executions were carried out; extrajudicial punishments included nearly 9,000 executions and 20,000 head shavings.

Raft of the Medusa, The—*see Le Radeau de la Méduse.*

Renault Celta 4 (1934-38): A mid-priced sedan with rear-wheel drive (4 cyl., 1463 c.c., 30 hp., 8 l/100 km).

roundup (in the context of *The Quiet Tides of Bordeaux*): A mass-arrest operation in a public place, or a private dwelling, or an internment centre. The purpose of roundups was to abduct and deport Jews by bus, lorry, or rail van to German extermination camps (approx. 1,660 Jews were thus deported from Bordeaux). Their purpose quickly evolved to ship communists, leftists, Gypsies, and foreign refugees who had been discharged or delegalized, to internment or concentration camps. As early as 1939, about ten French internment camps held some of the 450,000 refugees who had crossed over from Spain. The roundups were finally extended to any able-bodied individual who was sent to work in German companies. *See also* Service du travail obligatoire, tracking.

Royan, Charente-Maritime (Charente-Inférieure [1790-1941]): An English port from 1154 until 1451. It became a Protestant bastion and was subjugated and razed by Roman Catholics between 1623 and 1631. Royan was occupied by the Germans from 24 June 1940 until 17 April 1945; they had attempted surrender in August 1944. The harbour of Royan was attacked by the British and Canadians in August and September of 1944; the town was razed by 347 RAF bombers on 5 January 1945, killing 600, then bombed again and napalmed by 1,171 USAF bombers on 14 and 15 April 1945, killing another 400. The German HQ remained undamaged. Three days later, the fortress surrendered to French troops on 17-18 April 1945. *See also* Jonzac.

Saintes, Charente-Maritime (Charente-Inférieure [1790-1941]): The capital of Aquitaine in the 1st century, and a stage on the pilgrimage to St. James of Compostela. It was sporadically occupied by the English from 1271 until 1404, and disputed by Protestants and Roman Catholics between 1546 and 1579. It was occupied by the Germans from the end of June 1940 until 4 September 1944. *See also* Aquitaine[2].

Saint-Nazaire, Loire-Atlantique (Loire-Inférieure [1790-1957]): A former Breton port city that became French in 1532. It was occupied by the Germans from mid-June 1940 until 7 May 1945. A British naval and commando raid disabled the dry dock on 28 March 1942, and the city was firebombed, along with its trade school, by 1,000 RAF and USAF bombers on 28 February 1943, killing 479. It was the last German bastion in continental Europe, holding 30,000 men, and it was finally subjugated by the

Americans between 8 and 11 May 1945; the submarine base was undamaged. *See also* Triangular Trade.

San Sebastian, Basqueland: A port city that was the theatre of a failed revolt against the Spanish Republic from 19 to 28 July 1936. It was captured by the Spanish nationalist rebels on 13 September 1936.

Secours national (1914-18, 1939-44), or 'National Relief': An aid agency catering to victims of war, complementing the Red Cross. After June 1940, it was brought under the control of the head of state and used to liquidate properties seized from the Jews, and later from dissidents and black-market traffickers. It also managed revenues from the lottery, extra taxes, and takings from fêtes.

Semaine de Suzette, La (1905-40, 1946-60): A Roman-Catholic-inspired weekly with illustrations, for young girls.

Service du travail obligatoire (February 1943-July 1944), or 'Forced Labour Service': A French agency with the mandate to ship able-bodied workers to some 2,000 companies and factories in Germany; it was instituted after the departure of volunteer workers to Germany in 1940. Over a million salaried French people, of which 15,000 came from the Gironde Department, worked in Germany; 250,000 were POWs, 200,000 volunteers, and 650,000 conscripts (30,000 conscripts and volunteers never came back). Some 85,000 French residents evaded the Labour Service by joining the Resistance or by fleeing to Spain. This agency mirrored the 300 foreign work gangs forced to labour without pay in France from April 1939 until November 1945. Out of 15,000 Spaniards forced to work, 3,000 were assigned to the construction of Bordeaux's submarine base (70 of them died), but another 3,400 Spaniards and 2,000 German refugees escaped and joined the Resistance; the first French troops to enter Paris in August 1944 were of Spanish origin. *See also* roundup.

slava : The annual celebration, according to the Julian calendar, of the protector saint of a Serbian Orthodox home, performed on site by a pope (or by the head of the household); a probable integration of a pagan ritual from the Vintchan times.

Sleeping Beauty (1729), from the French *La Belle au bois dormant* (1697), by Charles Perrault (in the context of *The Quiet Tides of Bordeaux*): The 1935 French version of the same tale, by Henri Ghéon (real name Vangeon, 1875-1944). He was a doctor and playwright who converted back to Catholicism, and cofounded the fascist daily *Le Nouveau Siècle* (1925-28).

Spanish flu (1918-19): An Asian avian flu pandemic, causing 50,000,000 deaths, of which 400,000 were in France.

St. James of Compostela, Galicia, Spain: A pilgrimage site, dating back to the 11th century. After 1492, it became the third most important destination for Catholic pilgrimages. It was inspired by the Christians' desire to recover the Iberian Peninsula from the Moslems. The symbol of this pilgrimage is a scallop shell. (From the Spanish 'Santiago de Compostela', in which '[I]ago' refers to 'James' in English or 'Jacques' in French.)

Thérèse de Lisieux (Thérèse Martin, 1873-97): A Roman-Catholic saint canonized in 1925. She was a Carmelite theoretician of children's spirituality and of the holiness of ordinary people in their daily chores. Her writings were published posthumously, and she was made co-patron of missionaries in 1927 and of France in 1944. Lisieux is the second most important destination for Roman-Catholic pilgrimages in France, after Lourdes.

tidal bore: A relatively high sea wave that flows up the lower segment of a river at high tide; it may be used by surfers. The river resumes its normal flow back to the sea at the point where the strength of the upstream current has decreased to that of the downstream current. (In the context of *The Quiet Tides of Bordeaux*, it runs for about 140km and it was used by kayaking British commandos in a night attack on Bordeaux. *See also* Bordeaux, Gironde[1].)

Time of Cherries, The—see Le Temps des cerises.

tracking (in the context of *The Quiet Tides of Bordeaux*): The relentless tracking down of outlaws by special French and German police units during the Pétainist regime. In the Gironde Department, operations of this kind led to 806 executions of Resistance members and hostages, and to 1,300 deportations to Germany. Along with the regular jails and other facilities, such as 200 camps, the regime and the occupying powers had 900 internment centres at their disposal, of which 20, including Fort du Hâ, were in Gironde, 42 in Charente-Maritime, and 12 in Hautes-Pyrénées. *See also* roundup.

Triangular Trade (1510-1867): The sea trade between Europe, Africa, and the Americas, based on enslaved Africans—17,000,000 men and women may have been deported to America. Over one million died en route, and five million died within the first year of arrival. Port cities relevant to *The Quiet Tides of Bordeaux*, and involved in this trade, include Nantes, Saint-Nazaire, Bordeaux, and La Rochelle.

Wars of Religion (1520-1787): Nine armed economic and religious conflicts fought in France between Catholics and Protestants.

White Berets: A Roman-Catholic assistance group.

White Fathers (1868-): An antislavery Roman-Catholic missionary order working in Africa.

wood-gas unit: 1. A wood stove designed to generate combustible gas, and that may be fitted to an internal combustion engine (80,000 such stoves were built in 1941). 2. After 1900, a vehicle (barge, car, tank, etc.) with an engine fitted for wood-gas, used mainly during periods of fuel shortages.

–8Θ8Θ8–

About the author

J. L. F. Lambert was educated in Europe and North America. He established and directed the Terminology Unit of the Royal Canadian Mounted Police from 1975 to 1999, and he had the first English-French police dictionary posted on the Internet. He has served with the Department of Justice as a sworn translator in Ontario, and as an interpreter in Italy. His linguistic services were called upon by the Kent Constabulary for the Channel Tunnel operations, by the Cyprus Association of Translators, and by the hotel school of Santa Lucia, Cuba. He has taught terminology science at the University of Ottawa, and French at Collège de Jonquière in Gatineau, Quebec. He is the author of a glossary on plate tectonics, of an illustrated fingerprinting vocabulary, of a history of terminology science in antiquity (*Termcraft*, five stars from Clarion, 2014), and of unpublished short stories (incl. Sur les traces d'Hannibal, Special Jury Prize, Italian Week, Ottawa, 2007).

2eH Txt TNR 12 vsp 110 mrg 2 175 075

www.ingramcontent.com/pod-product-compliance
Lightning Source LLC
Chambersburg PA
CBHW060339100426
42812CB00003B/1054